MW00396693

# God Loves
## Experiencing Recovery on the Path of Grace

Eddie Snipes

# A book by:
# Exchanged Life Discipleship

Published by GES Book Publishing
Carrollton, GA

http://www.exchangedlife.com

Contact the author by visiting
http://www.eddiesnipes.com or
http://www.exchangedlife.com

Unless otherwise stated, the scripture in this book have
been taken from the New King James Version. Copyright
© 1982 by Thomas Nelson, Inc. Used by permission. All
rights reserved.


Picture Credits
Front cover photo(s) purchased at:
http://www.dreamstime.com

# Table of Contents

# My Testimony

I wrestled with whether I should reveal what type of addiction I had or not. My fear is that someone will look at my addiction and say, "That doesn't apply to me." I assure you that the same principles apply whether your addiction is behavioral, chemical, or physical. The flesh is the flesh, and the power of the Spirit overcomes the flesh. There is not one weakness in the flesh that isn't overcome by the promise of the Spirit.

One thing you have probably discovered is that those who don't have strong addictions do not understand the struggle. Most people say, "Just stop doing it." What they don't understand is that we have decided to just stop doing it. Many times. Suppose you are reading this and don't realize you also have a similar problem.

The greatest sin in the Bible is pride. Pride caused the fall of Satan, and the Bible says, "God resists the proud but gives grace to the humble." Do you have pride? Are you addicted to pride? Let someone offend you and see if pride isn't an addiction. If someone takes credit for your work, what is your response? If someone insults you, what is your response?

What if someone said, "Just stop being proud?" Don't feel insulted when someone hurts your pride. Don't be upset when the person who works less than you gets a promotion. Or someone gets praised for what you have done. Or someone makes a snide comment that stirs anger in your gut. Just stop being proud and there won't be a problem.

What about, "Just don't worry." Does that make worry go away? Does being told to quit being afraid make fear dispel? Or being told to quit eating make you stop snacking? What about spending, perfectionism, being a workaholic, feelings of insecurity, or any number of other human weaknesses. We all have addictions, but most are accepted by society. Or at least they are tolerated.

Most harmful behavior is learned early in life. My situation was no different. Around the age of eight, a friend of mine had an older brother store boxes in his room while he was away at college. Several of those boxes contained pornography. To curious young boys, this was a discovery of hidden treasure. But that treasure was cursed. We visited the boxes often to explore the contents of hundreds of magazines.

Several years back I was reading articles from the American Psychology Association. One of the articles cited research from the brains of those with sexual addictions and deviancies. It was discovered that almost all those with abnormal sexuality had over-developed parts of the brain that are responsible for sexual response. From this discovery, many assumptions have been put forth. One includes the theory of the 'gay gene'. However, it wasn't only homosexuals that had abnormal brain development. It showed up in almost all sexual behavior that was considered abnormal.

If we honestly look at the evidence, it should be clear that this brain development is a response to overstimulation. Add to the mix the fact that most of the people studied were linked to either abuse or sexual exposure early in life. In other words, sexual stimulation was excessive during the years when the brain was growing and developing.

This can be observed in other areas as well. Why do children who are verbally and physically abused have abnormal temper and behavioral issues? Why do kids who see violence grow up to become violent? Or those with early childhood trauma become fearful adults? Name the abnormal behavior and it can usually be linked back to a specific childhood incident or series of incidents.

Phobias, obsessions, addictions, and behaviors are almost always the result of alterations or unusual developments of the brain.

It's important to understand this because it explains why an outsider can see a behavior and wonder why someone doesn't just stop, but the person suffering can't. Their brain has developed with a bent toward a certain behavior. Often the brain is dependent upon a certain stimulation in order to feel normal. Drugs affect the brain in much this same way.

This is why I decided to abandon pornography in my teen years, but could not. From the age of eight until thirteen, I consumed pornography without any thought of stopping. But when I became a Christian, my perspective changed. I no longer wanted to fill my mind with lust, but instead had a desire to be pure. I did not feel guilty for the past because I had been forgiven. I set my sights on the future and wanted to be the godly person I knew God called me to be.

But there was a problem. My brain was stuck in the past and unable to abandon what I had conditioned it to do.

Once the emotions of my new found faith began to fade, strange desires began emerging. In the past these desires weren't unusual, but now I had a desire of the flesh that conflicted with the desire for life. I decided not to go back to porn, but the desire kept growing stronger. In a moment of weakness I gave in.

I felt bad and vowed to never look again. But soon the desires returned. Even though I tried to resist, it was like something captured my mind and dragged me into a fog of obsession. A fog is the perfect description. The world lost focus and all I could see was desire. The craving was so overwhelming that I could not think of anything else. The fog never went away until I indulged to gratify this craving.

Now I was wracked with guilt. I had broken my vow to God and indulged in a porn binge. I renewed my promise to keep my mind pure, but this was a commitment beyond my ability. The fog would return. It might be a few days or a month, but when the fog rolled in, all I could think about was getting alone and feeding the flesh. It would be satisfied – by my willing participation or by irresistible urges against my will.

One time I was reading my Bible and felt as though I had finally escaped. I felt renewed and forgiven. As I read, the fog rolled in without warning and without provocation. I tried to resist, but it was too strong for me. After wrestling against it and knowing I was losing, I closed my Bible and went for a fix.

This was one of the most hopeless feelings I had ever known. If I was not safe while reading my Bible and doing spiritual things, what hope did I have? If the beast of my flesh could take over my mind while reading scripture, all was lost indeed.

For the next twenty-years I fought this losing battle. I was active in church and tried to overcome by serving God. I even preached in the youth. To this day I meet people who thought I was a good example of a Christian youth, but no one knew the secret war I was losing.

In my mid-twenties I married. I found that my problem wasn't merely a desire for sex. It was a craving for porn. I hid my addiction from my wife and had to find ways to feed the addiction without the shame of being discovered. This bred mistrust in our relationship. She knew I was not being honest, but didn't know why.

After nearly twenty years of trying to overcome, I gave up. I concluded that I was just wired this way and there was nothing I could do to change this. In a way, this was true – but overcoming was within my grasp, though I didn't know it.

For three years I quit going to church. Christianity didn't work, so I decided to get away from anything that would remind me of my guilt. I hid my addiction, but I did nothing to curb it. God was not in my thoughts and I even found myself wondering if He really existed. Though there were evidences that proved many ways He was working in my life, I found my inability to overcome to be stronger evidence than what I had experienced. It didn't matter anyway. God had to be angry at me for sinning so many times.

Though I pushed faith out of my life and had no exposure to Christianity for almost three years, I didn't feel peace. I convinced myself I could forget godliness, but nothing satisfied me. I felt more miserable than before. I buried myself in my job and set my focus on building a career. I excelled, got promotions, and moved up in the corporate world. I set a five-year goal and achieved it. I landed the job I was sure would make me happy. For five years I did nothing but build my skills, get job experience, and train for the position I wanted.

In April of 1998 I achieved that goal. I climbed the mountain of success, and when I crested the pinnacle, I realized that nothing of value was up there. I had climbed to the top and my success was the biggest let down of my life. Certainly I could have set higher goals, but if there was nothing on top of this mountain, there would be nothing on top of the next one.

That was the day everything in my world crashed. People praised me for doing well. My future in the job market looked bright. I had a new home. The people around me thought I had it all together. But I knew otherwise. It was all vanity – empty and meaningless.

I took several days to withdraw to myself and try to find answers. In my heart, I knew God had the answer, but since I had abandoned God, I felt He had abandoned me.

My office was in Roswell, GA, and I wasn't far from a national park. I decided to drive to the park and take a walk to clear my head. The thought occurred to me that I should pray, but God seemed far away. I doubted if He was within a million miles of me.

After a quick drive, I strolled through the wooded trails. It was quiet and few people were around. It was a perfect place to clear my head. I attempted to pray, but God was nowhere to be found, so I spent most of my walk complaining to myself. I do remember praying one thing, "Why, God? Why can't I keep any area of my life under control?" No answer.

Once I finished the long walk, I headed back. Nothing changed. Everything still looked as hopeless as before and my prayer was useless. I just wasted my time.

The next day I felt compelled to walk in the park again. I saw no good reason, but I still longed for something. After I settled in at the office, I headed to the park for another walk. Again I walked and complained, prayed a little into the air, but felt no sense of relief. My long walk came to an end and I headed back to the office.

Emptiness continued to consume me and I couldn't settle my soul. When the drawing I felt would not give me rest, I made the trip again to the park. "Why, God. Why is my life so meaningless? I can't control myself and I can't break free of this addiction. I can't live the Christian life. I've tried, but can't do it." I walked, prayed, and lamented on the hilltop trails of the park.

Then something unexpected happened. It's hard to put into words, but I'll give a glimpse into my experience. It was almost as if I were in a cloud. I could see nothing as far as the physical world around me. The feeling of God's presence flooded my being as if a wave washed both over and through me. In an instant, scriptures came to mind that I don't remember reading or even being aware of. Then it felt like chains fell from my mind and I felt as if I had been set free from my addiction. I don't know if this experience lasted for a moment, an hour, or many hours. Time seemed irrelevant.

When the forest came back into view, I felt completely changed. I returned to my walking as I truly prayed for the first time in recent memory. As I prayed, I said, "Lord, I know this isn't just for me." I had a sudden awareness of a new purpose in life. I considered my career and realized it was no longer my concern.

I left the park that day a different person. For weeks, maybe even months, my head swarmed with thoughts, ideas, and scriptures. In time they settled into a solid foundation. I also made a few flawed assumptions as well.

My Testimony

Another thing I instantly knew when emerging from the park was the need to verify my experience against scripture. It was as if God was challenging me to confirm what was revealed by comparing it to the word. Again in my spirit I felt this truth and I prayed, "If this is really of God and the things I saw in my mind were of God," and I knew they were, "then I'll be able to affirm each of these with scripture."

I went home and found a Bible concordance. I began to do word searches to find the scriptures that came to mind. And there were not just a few. For hours I combed through the concordance and the Bible and 100% of the things given to me were waiting to be discovered in the text of the scriptures.

There were many, but one that was the most meaningful was this. I had spent all my life trying to make myself righteous - and failing. I was depending on myself becoming better and making myself good by personal effort. But the Lord revealed to me that my efforts, even my best goodness, was filthy in His sight. But along with that was this realization, that God clothes me with His righteousness and covers me with His goodness. That is how I become beautiful in His eyes.

At home I found these three passages:

**Isaiah 64:6**
But we are all like an unclean thing,
And all our righteousnesses are like filthy rags;
We all fade as a leaf,
And our iniquities, like the wind,
Have taken us away.


**Isaiah 61:10**
I will greatly rejoice in the Lord,
My soul shall be joyful in my God;
For He has clothed me with the garments of salvation,
He has covered me with the robe of righteousness,
As a bridegroom decks himself with ornaments,
And as a bride adorns herself with her jewels.


**2 Corinthians 5:21**
For He made Him who knew no sin to be sin for us, that we might become the righteousness of God in Him.

As I searched, discoveries like these continued to affirm all the things God revealed to me that day. How could God want to have fellowship with a miserable porn addict? It was simple. He put to death the flesh with its passions and desires. He had no desire to make the old flesh appear better by perfuming it and trying to make my sins look better. He nailed these things to His cross by becoming sin for me, and in turn, He gave me His righteousness. It was the exchanged life. I exchanged my sin for His righteousness.

Now I'm righteous because He has covered me with the beauty of His righteousness. No longer did I have to worry that God was looking at Eddie the porn addict. God was looking at the righteousness of Christ - a perfect righteousness that was complete and lacking nothing. And corrupted by nothing, for it is the righteousness of Christ.

As amazing as these discoveries were, they were only a small taste of what God intended to reveal - and continues to reveal. But first God had to build my life on the faith He had given me, and then shake that faith so any other confidences would fall away.

One concern I have when sharing this testimony is that people will think they have to have this exact experience in order to be delivered. Two things we'll explore in this book is how you can experience the promise of God's Holy Spirit and how to overcome in everyday life.

For months I felt untouchable by porn. But I was riding the wave of emotion, and this is not the power of the Spirit. Being freed from my chains was exhilarating, but true freedom came when I learned to walk in the Spirit.

Three months later the desires returned. Again I found myself wrestling against the flesh, but this time I had a secure foundation. I understood that God had set me free, but I now had to learn how to walk in that freedom. I wish I could say that I never again gave into temptation, but I did. Though I never was engulfed in the fog as before, I gave into my desire on occasion over the next few years.

This is why I feel it is important to warn people that they will fail. It is not unusual to struggle against the flesh, but you will learn to overcome. I still had to learn how to walk in the Spirit and reckon (or account) myself dead to sin. I had no one to guide me and I made many mistakes. Because I had a lot of false assumptions, this caused unnecessary pain and set me up for unnecessary failure.

It is my goal to share these principles with you so you can experience the victory of the Christian life. When you fail, don't hide from God. He already knew you would fail and has already set His work in motion to guide you back into His perfect will.

Failure shows us what doesn't work. We are human, and though we'd love to get it right the first time, God knows that we are easily distracted and wander off course. He is called the Good Shepherd because He protects the sheep and guides them back to the right path. The Good Shepherd protects and guides the sheep. He does not beat the sheep and cast them away.

When you fail, learn from the mistake. What led you into the flesh? The road to failure sometimes is trying to do good by human effort. It doesn't always begin with what we think of as failure. Trying to make ourselves godly is just as much an act of the flesh as it is to give into our addiction.

God's desire is for you to experience Him in the fullness of joy. Your relationship with God is the most important part of overcoming. As you learn to walk with God, the weakness of the flesh loses its grip. When you fail, remember that the righteous falls and gets up again. You are righteous in Christ, so when you blow it, get up and trust again in His love. It's the goodness of God that leads you to repentance.

God is not limited by your addictions. Your failure is not a barrier to God. The only barrier between you and victory is unbelief. Do you believe God will keep His word? Do you believe God's promises? Do you believe God's power can overcome sin and weakness?

When you fail, the enemy will whisper in your ear and tell you that God rejects you. He will say that you have sinned too many times. He will say that you are running out of chances. He will say that God is looking at your failures.

God has declared your acceptance in Christ. He has declared that you are forgiven and sin has been paid – all sin. He has declared that His strength is made perfect in your weakness. God loves you in the pit of failure, and He rejoices when you allow Him to take you out of the miry pit and put you on the rock of Christ.

God loves you as you are and where you are. The only question is: can you recognize His love and can you trust in His grace?

It's time to start your journey of recovery and rejoice in the power God has given to you that enables you to receive His promises. Walk by faith and trust in His power to overcome your weakness. Your addiction has no power over God's Spirit – if you walk by faith. Faith is the only barrier God has placed upon Himself.

The promise is already yours. Believe, receive it, and begin your walk of victory!

# God Loves the Addict

If you are struggling with addiction, you have a great advantage in life that few others have. The Bible says that God is near to those who are broken and the contrite heart He will never reject. Those who are defeated by addiction or have an out-of-control life often have eyes to see what others can't.

The person who has it all together feels self-sufficient and only looks to themselves for goodness. But God rejects human goodness and only accepts what is given to us through Him. The person who feels like they have it together will never have eyes to see the greatness of God's power. Through your addiction, God has already revealed the valuelessness of human goodness. And this is the first step in looking outside of ourselves and toward Christ.

When you surrender your weaknesses to Christ, you receive God's strength. When you surrender your failure, you receive God's success. When you give Him your sins, you receive the righteousness of God. You are perfect in Him when you give your imperfections to the Lord! Rejoice that God has brought you to the place to see this amazing gift of grace that few fully realize.

When going through struggles, we will experience a lot of failure. The Bible says that a righteous man will fall, but will get up again.[1] Scripture does not teach that righteous people don't fall. The problem is that when we fall, we feel like a failure and do not consider ourselves as righteous.

In ourselves, we are not righteous, for according to the apostle who wrote two-thirds of the New Testament, "In me, that is in my flesh, nothing good dwells."[2] The Apostle Paul goes on to say how that he desires to do good (righteousness), but how to perform it is not found in him. His efforts could not produce righteousness. The man God used to teach the church the truths of God's word acknowledged that he has no power to do good or create righteousness.

The same is true for you. You fail when your weaknesses are in control of your life. You experience victory when God's Spirit is

---

[1] Proverbs 24:16
[2] Romans 7:18

allowed to empower your life. Your natural tendency is to serve your flesh – that part of you that craves to be satisfied. Everyone is addicted to the flesh, but some addictions are more evident than others. People don't consider selfishness to be an addiction, but it is. Even pride is an addiction to satisfy our egos and create self-worth through human achievement.

Those who struggle with addictions such as pornography, alcohol, drugs, gambling, and other clearly destructive behaviors have an advantage over everyone else. You recognize your need. Hidden sins of the heart are just as harmful to our souls, but these are so subtle and socially acceptable that few recognize their need.

Jesus gave an illustration that explains this. He said a Pharisee (the highest religious leader of that culture) went into the temple to pray. When he walked in, he saw a tax collector. Tax collectors were considered the most wicked people of the culture because they could legally rob people. They were required to collect a certain amount of taxes for the Roman government, but they could add as much extra as they wanted, and people had to pay that amount. If they wanted, they could bankrupt their enemies and sap any amount of wealth they desired from the town's people. They were the most hated people of Jesus' day.

The religious Pharisee looked down at the tax collector and prayed, "I thank you that I'm not like this worthless man. I pay tithes of everything I own. I pray every day. I fast regularly. I keep the law to the letter."

The tax collector would not even lift his eyes off the ground. In the anguish of his heart he said, "Lord, have mercy on me, for I'm a sinner."

Jesus said, "The tax collector walked out of the temple justified, but not the Pharisee."

You see, it doesn't matter how vile your life has been, who you are, or what you have done. It is not you who creates righteousness. You are given righteousness. God does not deal with you based on your failures, but based on His abilities. He doesn't judge you based on your sins, but based on the righteousness of Christ. Take to heart the words of **2 Corinthians 5:21**

For He made Him who knew no sin *to be* sin for us, that we might become the righteousness of God in Him.

In Christ, you are the righteousness of God. Your sins – including your addictions of the past and failures of the future – were laid to Christ's account. And His perfection was laid to your account. Whether you are a tax collector, preacher, minister, addict, prostitute, drunkard, good church boy or girl, average Joe, or any other person, you have the same need. Justification is to those who look to Christ and say, "Have mercy on me, a sinner."

Once you are in Christ, the picture changes. No longer do you look to yourself and say, "I am a sinner," but now you look to Christ and by faith say, "I am the righteousness of God in Him."

This is a hard concept to believe, but until you have faith in this promise, you are stuck in the flesh. The flesh has nothing good in it. As the Apostle Paul said when he looked to his own efforts, "Nothing good dwells in me, that is in my flesh. Who will rescue me from this body of death?" Yet he then declared, "I thank God through Jesus Christ my Lord. Through my flesh I serve sin, but through my mind I serve the law of God."

This is the exchanged life. When you look to yourself, sin is the only thing you can produce. Even your good deeds are ultimately self-serving. But when you look to Christ, the mind is transformed by faith into His likeness and the Spirit of God is placed within you. Only then can your mind serve the law of God. It is not you who serves the law by human effort. It is the transformed life that naturally does the things that are righteous because we are trusting in Christ and receiving both His righteousness and the power of His Spirit.

When you live according to the flesh – human effort – you will fail. When you live in the Spirit, success is a guarantee. It is not you who changes your life, but God who works in you to produce the fruit of the Spirit – which is the love of God, peace, joy, patience, kindness, goodness, faith, gentleness, and self-control.[3]

Do you need self-control? If an addiction is dominating your life, self-control is a desperate need. These things come through the fruit of the Spirit. They are produced by God in your life, not by you trying harder. The Bible says that we are changed into Christ's likeness as we behold His glory.[4] The Bible does not say that we are

---

[3] Galatians 5:22-23
[4] 2 Corinthians 3:18

changed into Christ's image by religious efforts, more discipline, or by trying harder.

Some people can alter certain behaviors by learning how to become dependent upon other behaviors. They change a destructive addiction for a less destructive addiction. For others, this does not work. The addictions they wrestle against are too strong and the drawing too great.

While behavioral change may help some in this life, what true value are we getting if our efforts are passing away and have no eternal significance? Take advantage of the exposure of your weakness and fulfill the need with God's power. Don't just cover it with something else.

The Apostle Paul said, "I will glory in my weakness, for in weakness the power of God rests upon me." He not only discovered his weakness, but he learned how to use that weakness to receive the power of God. He didn't just learn to cope; he learned to receive. He received victory in this life, but also received the hope for eternity. Eternal significance is more important than recovery. Yet it is also true that the Spirit, who gives us eternal significance, is the power of recovery.

When you fail, do not grovel in defeat. Let it be a reminder that you are weak, and take advantage of this weakness to learn to trust in your dependence upon Christ.

God does not seethe with anger when you blow it. In fact, the one who sees their weakness is closer to experiencing the grace of God than the pious church member who believes they have no need. A Christian who depends on their own strength is farther from experiencing God's power than an addict crying out in the midst of failure.

In the flesh, you are always out of God's will. In the Spirit, you are always in God's will. It begins with a relationship with Christ. Let me stop for a moment and discuss what it means to be in Christ.

# In Christ.

When this book refers to being in Christ, I am speaking of the person who has received Christ as Savior and are born again. The term 'born again' is what Jesus used to explain the new life of the

Spirit. We are born with a sinful nature through Adam. At the end of this book I'll give resources I have written where this is explained more fully, but I will summarize it here.

According to the Bible, when someone puts their faith in Christ for salvation, God transforms that person into a new creation. Their old nature is put to death in Christ, and they are raised as a new creation with a new nature, one that is born by the Spirit. This is the new birth. It is to have a new life, born by the Holy Spirit. At the same time, the scriptures teach that God places His Spirit within us and we become the temple of God.

By faith in Christ, we give Jesus our old life – sins and all. We put our trust in Him and receive His new life – righteousness and all. All our sins have been taken out of the way, because Jesus nailed it to the cross. The sinful nature that once dominated our minds has been put to death in Christ, and we receive a new nature whose life is in Christ.

How does one know they are in Christ? Do you trust in your efforts? What does your hope rest upon? Do you believe you must do something in order to be accepted by God or to remain acceptable to God? If so, your faith is in yourself and not in Christ.

A Christian is one who rests his or her hopes fully upon Christ. His work is our confidence. His righteousness is our righteousness. His crucifixion took away our sin. His life is our life. A Christian, according to the Bible, is someone who rests their hope fully upon the completed work of Christ. We are righteous through Him, apart from what we do or have done. We have life in Him. We are acceptable in God's eyes because we are in Christ. As the Bible states, we have no confidence in the flesh, but rest our hope fully upon Him.

If you cannot say that you have a heart that rests in Christ, give Him your life as you are and receive His life in its fullness. Just pray and invite Him into your life and give all you are to Him. You don't need a model prayer, for God responds to your heart, not your words. The Bible says that if we confess Him as Lord, God will give us the gift of salvation. Your words are not what saves you. By faith, we believe, God accounts us as righteous, and He does the work to crucify the old nature and give us a new nature. Consider **Romans 10:9-11**

[9] that if you confess with your mouth the Lord Jesus and believe in your heart that God has raised Him from the dead,

you will be saved.

<sup>10</sup> For with the heart one believes unto righteousness, and with the mouth confession is made unto salvation.

<sup>11</sup> For the Scripture says, "Whoever believes on Him will not be put to shame."

Confess Him as Lord and receive His life. From this position of faith we have the promise that God will transform us into His likeness. The process of transformation is a lifelong endeavor, but each day brings the life of Christ out more and more in our thoughts, actions, and attitudes.

# What if I Blow it?

Perhaps a better question would be, what happens *when* I blow it. When someone experiences the life of Christ for the first time, there is often an emotional drive that makes sin seem like a distant memory. It's as if we have risen above our problems and they cannot touch us.

This won't last. There will be other times in life when the move of God energizes us with strong emotions, but this too won't last. God does not want you to be dependent upon emotions. God wants you to trust in Him and rest fully upon His power. It takes no faith to rest in a strong feeling. But we are called to walk by faith and not by sight – or any other physical means.

When emotions fade, you will have to learn how to work out your own salvation. Consider **Philippians 2:12-13**

<sup>12</sup> Therefore, my beloved, as you have always obeyed, not as in my presence only, but now much more in my absence, work out your own salvation with fear and trembling;

<sup>13</sup> for it is God who works in you both to will and to do for *His* good pleasure.

Work out – not for salvation. You have received salvation, now you need to learn how to walk according to your new nature. Those who have addictive behaviors will see these habits rising up and warring against our minds, trying to regain control.

When you begin walking by faith, you will blow it more times than not. You have a lifetime of habit to work through. From birth until now, you have walked by what you see and feel. During that time, you have acquired an addiction that serves the flesh in some way, and your flesh will not go quietly into that dark night.

Regardless of how you feel now, prepare yourself to respond in a healthy way once you blow it. You will sin. You will fall back into addictive behaviors. You'll then feel like a failure and frustration will tell you that its hopeless. You will also feel like God is angry because you didn't measure up to His standards.

You know what? You cannot measure up to God's standards. That is the reason Christ gave Himself to rescue you from sin. If you could measure up, Christ would not have died. God would have given you the power to keep the law through methods and procedures. Instead, the Bible says that the law serves to condemn us, reveal the weakness of the flesh, make the entire world guilty before God, and direct us to Christ.

Scripture teaches that the law failed to make us righteous because of the weakness of the flesh. The law is not weak; the flesh is weak because of fallen human nature. Therefore, anything dependent upon human effort is weak and destined for failure. Overcoming addictions is the process of learning how to wean our confidence off the flesh and onto Christ. It is learning how to use the weakness of our flesh to reveal the strength of God.

When you fail, don't grovel in guilt, but let it be a reminder that you are completely dependent upon the power of Christ to transform you. When you step into a fleshly way of thinking, addictions and other works of the flesh overcome you. The answer isn't guilt, but stepping out of the flesh and into the Spirit where God's power is given.

God is not dealing with you based on who you are, but who you will be when you stand before Him complete in Christ. While you are falling, God is already working in your life to produce His good pleasure. And what greater pleasure could God have in your life than to make you holy and able to commune in fellowship with Himself? That is the purpose of salvation. The Lord desires for you to become partakers of His nature so you can fully inherit His kingdom. And nothing shows the power of God more than to take someone who cannot overcome the flesh and transform that person into a trophy of His grace!

God delights in showing His power in the lives of those who are incapable of being holy.

When I was pursuing my desire for sin, God was setting the stage for me to receive His blessings. Though I had given up completely and decided to live for the cravings of my flesh, God was blessing my life based on what He was about to do – not based on my goodness. I had no righteousness. Yet God dealt with me based on His grace and not based on my failures.

The same is true for you. It's God's good pleasure to give you His kingdom.[5] In order to give you the kingdom and make you a joint-heir with Christ,[6] God must bring you into a position to receive it. God *does not* pick out those who have achieved a religious standard and make them into heirs. God picks those who cannot do in order to show Himself strong on their behalf, and He makes them righteous. Then God rewards us for being possessors of His righteousness, not for becoming righteous in ourselves.

God's pleasure is to take your failure, bury it with Christ, and empower you with life and His Spirit. His goal is to empty you of the flesh so He can fill you with the Spirit. The sad reality is that most people feel confident in themselves and never see the need to empty their lives of self-effort so they can receive God's power and the fullness of the Spirit. But you as the addict have that realization.

For you, this is good news indeed. If you are reading this, it is likely that you cannot overcome and fully recognize your need. You already know that you can't do this by human effort. You've probably tried for years, but cannot overcome. Instead of feeling self-righteous, you probably feel defeated and unworthy. Take time to thank God for this revelation! God's strength is made perfect in weakness because those who are weak recognize their dependency on Christ.

When you have no confidence in the flesh or your efforts, you are now in a position to be Christ confident and experience the fullness of God's power. When God is your strength, nothing is

---

[5] Luke 12:32
[6] Romans 8:17

impossible. And you will have the perspective that understands how to look to Him alone through every walk of this life of faith.

# The Love of God

The love of God is a hard concept to grasp. This shouldn't be so, but we naturally gravitate toward a performance based view of life. In society, our performance is the measure of worth. Not only that, it has to be the right kind of performance. A day laborer may work his fingers to the bone and perform at the highest level, but society won't praise him. Society bases performance on image. Those who perform in ways that create wealth are respected. Those who perform well in sports, acting, or any other profession are rewarded with both money and respect.

Most people even have a performance based family life. If we act in ways that please parents, spouses, siblings, or other family members, we are respected. But if we fall short what happens? We are made to feel as if we are a disappointment.

Biblical Christianity is a non-performance based acceptance by God. I say 'biblical Christianity' because many religions based upon Christianity fall short of this truth. In fact, most Christians fall short of this truth. Speak to the average church member and ask what pleases God. You will likely hear things like doing good works, keeping God's commandments, giving to the church, going to church, and any number of other do's.

The truth is that God's acceptance is based on what Christ has accomplished and is never based on what we do. In Christ we have victory in life. Consider all the things guaranteed to those who are in Christ. We have life.[7] God anoints us with His Spirit and establishes us in Christ.[8] God always leads us to triumph.[9] We are a new creation and have a new life where old things have passed away.[10] We are reconciled to God.[11] We are more than conquerors.[12] We have overcome the world and have victory.[13] We have been sanctified.[14] In Christ we have no condemnation.[15]

---

[7] Romans 6:11
[8] 2 Corinthians 1:21
[9] 2 Corinthians 2:14
[10] 2 Corinthians 5:17
[11] 2 Corinthians 5:19
[12] Romans 8:37
[13] 1 John 5:4-5

Check out the scripture references listed in the footnotes. You will notice an important truth. All of these things are past tense. In other words, God has already accomplished these things for you and your only call is to walk in God's accomplished works by faith.

Do you feel sanctified? Sanctification is something that has been declared holy and set apart for God. Is this what you feel? Most likely you don't feel holy or sanctified, but this is an accomplished fact and not based on feelings or performance.

In Christ, we have no condemnation. So if we feel condemned, that guilt is not coming from God. If you sin, you have no condemnation. Don't forget that you cannot be righteous by human effort. Self-created righteousness only serves to make us feel good about ourselves, but it does nothing to make us right before God. In fact, when men declared their good deeds before Christ, good works they performed in Jesus' name, Christ called them workers of sin.[16]

The truth is that when we commit sin, it is an act of the flesh. It's of the flesh and the flesh can only produce sin. The flesh can never produce the righteousness of God.[17] When we do good works by our own efforts, it is a work of the flesh and cannot produce righteousness.

Good works by human effort is a declaration of man's independence from God. It is to rebel against God's word that He must be our righteousness. It is to count the sacrifice of Christ as worthless and to declare that we can do it on our own. It is man's effort to satisfy himself apart from God. It is to put our faith in our flesh because we don't believe God is able to complete righteousness without us.

When we sin, it is an act of the flesh as we declare ourselves independent of God. It is to say that God's promise to be our exceedingly great reward as insufficient. Willful sinning is to declare God's promise to satisfy our souls with the river of His pleasures as lacking and worthless. It is to put our faith in our flesh to satisfy us because we don't believe God.

---

[14] Hebrews 10:10
[15] Romans 8:1
[16] Matthew 7:22-23
[17] John 3:6

Do you see a commonality between the good deeds of the flesh and the sinful desires of the flesh? There is no difference. In our eyes they are different, but in God's eyes, an act of the flesh is of the flesh – whether we think it is sinful or good. If it is of the flesh, it is flesh. If it is not of God, it is of man. According to the Bible, the flesh and the Spirit can never agree and are at war with each other.[18]

It's important for you to realize this vital truth, for once you understand this, you can recognize that your struggle is no more a barrier to righteousness than the pious church member who does all the right things outwardly, but never recognizes their need for God's righteousness. Or as the Bible says about the religious leaders of Christ's day, "While seeking to establish their own righteousness, they did not find the righteousness of God."[19]

Regardless of what type of addiction you are struggling with, it boils down to this simple principle. What is of the flesh is the flesh, and what is of the Spirit is Spirit. The answer is not to conform your flesh to a righteous standard. The answer is to look to Christ and allow Him to establish you in His righteousness. Then you are submitting to the Holy Spirit to give you His power to abide in Christ.

# Does God hate sinners?

You have likely seen the banners declaring that God hates gays, or God hates America, or God hates sinners. Some go as far as to say that God rejoices when sinners die. You may have even seen these things on picket signs at funerals of high profile celebrities by a vocal group that seeks constant attention. Consider this truth in **Ezekiel 33:11a**

> Say to them: '*As* I live,' says the Lord GOD, 'I have no pleasure in the death of the wicked, but that the wicked turn from his way and live.

This truth was so important that God said it twice in Ezekiel.[20] Does God hate gays? Does God hate sinners? Those who declare

---

[18] Galatians 5:17
[19] Romans 10:3
[20] Ezekiel 18:32 and 33:11

The Love of God

such things are blind to their own sins. The truth is that sin is sin. The original sin is pride. Satan was the highest angel in heaven and perfect until pride arose in him. His goal was to be independent of God and then exalt himself. And what was Adam's fall? The temptation was, "You will be like God." Satan tempted Adam with pride by luring him to seek independence from God. Pride caused his fall and consequences followed Adam's attempt to become independent of God.

Who struggles with pride? Perhaps a better question would be, who doesn't? When I do something right, I'm proud of my efforts or accomplishment. When I look down on someone's sin, I am enthroning myself and exalting my self-righteous attitude over the other person. Just as the Pharisee felt proud of his righteousness and condemned the sinner in front of him, the Christian falls into this same trap when they look down on homosexuality, addicts, thieves, or other sinners as though they are worse than themselves.

But which is worse? Homosexuality or pride? Drug addiction or self-righteousness? The truth is that the ground at the foot of the cross is level. We all are in need of God's mercy and His power to overcome our weakness of the flesh.

I'm driving home this point because I want the reader to recognize that there are no hierarchical sins. What is big in our eyes is not in God's. What is small in our eyes is still sin in God's eyes. And the Lord does not seek our condemnation, but our deliverance.

When the religious leaders brought a woman caught in adultery to Jesus, they said, "The law says she must die. What do you say?"

A few questions come to mind immediately. First, where was the man she was with? That is the nature of religion. The very people trying to condemn others excuse the sins that are inconvenient to their agendas. No one keeps the law, yet they try to use the law against others. Jesus proved this truth as we'll soon see.

The second question is why did they feel the need to bring the woman to Jesus? They didn't acknowledge His authority and certainly could have executed the woman without His input.

They came to Jesus because they knew that His desire is always for mercy. The Bible says that Jesus was God in the flesh and full of grace and truth.[21] Even Jesus' critics understood His heart of grace.

---

[21] John 1:1, John 1:14

They knew the law condemned the woman, but they also thought the law could condemn grace.

Jesus stooped down and started drawing in the dirt. I envision Him drawing out words like, Adultery – lust is adultery in the heart. Greed – idolatry in the heart. Covetousness – stealing in the heart. Jesus often showed our need for grace by pointing out that even if we don't show outward behaviors, sinning in our heart makes us just as guilty as the physical act.

They grew impatient and said, "Jesus, the law says she must be stoned, what do *you* say."

After a few more impatient demands for an answer, Jesus stood up and said, "Whoever is without sin, let him cast the first stone."

Those who boasted of their abilities to keep the law looked at Jesus' words on the ground and their own consciences convicted them. One by one they walked away until Jesus was alone with the woman. "Where are your accusers?"

"There are none," she answered Jesus.

"Neither do I condemn you. Go and sin no more."

Do you see the glorious message of grace? While the law and others stand as our accusers, God is the only one not accusing. While we think God is our accuser, the truth is that He alone offers grace. God rescues you from sin and then gives you His Spirit. When you are walking in the Spirit, sin has no power and you can go and sin no more.

When you are in the flesh, sin is inevitable. This is true whether you have evil intentions or good ones. In the Spirit, you are abiding in Christ's righteousness and in Him there is no sin or condemnation.

Whether your sin is substance related, sexual, or anything else, there is no condemnation. God loves the sinner. Every child of God was once a sinner rescued by grace. God is not looking for those who can measure up to a godly standard. Jesus came to seek and save those who are lost.

# God Loves the Sinner

Let's look at several passages that should be a comfort to all who struggle. First look at **Romans 5:6-8**

<sup>6</sup> For when we were still without strength, in due time Christ died for the ungodly.

<sup>7</sup> For scarcely for a righteous man will one die; yet perhaps for a good man someone would even dare to die.

<sup>8</sup> But God demonstrates His own love toward us, in that while we were still sinners, Christ died for us.

**1 John 3:16a**

By this we know love, because He laid down His life for us.

The requirement for qualifying for God's mercy is that we are a sinner. Since that fits everyone, grace is available to all. But those who are focused on religious efforts and good performance can never see their need for grace. God loved us while we were sinners. God loves the sinner. Let's see a few more passages that shore up this truth. Look at **John 3:16-19**

<sup>16</sup> "For God so loved the world that He gave His only begotten Son, that whoever believes in Him should not perish but have everlasting life.

<sup>17</sup> "For God did not send His Son into the world to condemn the world, but that the world through Him might be saved.

<sup>18</sup> "He who believes in Him is not condemned; but he who does not believe is condemned already, because he has not believed in the name of the only begotten Son of God.

<sup>19</sup> "And this is the condemnation, that the light has come into the world, and men loved darkness rather than light, because their deeds were evil.

Let's also bring **1 John 2:15** in for comparison:

<sup>15</sup> Do not love the world or the things in the world. If anyone loves the world, the love of the Father is not in him.

God so loved the world – those who did not have the love of God and were opposed to God – that He gave. Christ came to reach out to those who were living in opposition to God. The Bible says that those in the flesh are enemies with God. Yet God loved those who were His enemies so much that He gave all to rescue us from sin. That sin could be in the form of addictions, or just a selfish lifestyle. Look at one other passage that seals the deal, **1 John 4:8-10**

<sup>8</sup> He who does not love does not know God, for God is love.
<sup>9</sup> In this the love of God was manifested toward us, that God has sent His only begotten Son into the world, that we might live through Him.
<sup>10</sup> In this is love, not that we loved God, but that He loved us and sent His Son *to be* the propitiation for our sins.

...

<sup>16</sup> And we have known and believed the love that God has for us. God is love, and he who abides in love abides in God, and God in him.

God is love. Nothing captures the truth of grace more than this one statement. God does not love you because of the good you have done. God does not withdraw love because of the bad you have done. God loves because that is His essence. The word for God's love is agape, which means the love of God, outward focused, self-sacrificing, unconditional love.

God loves you because that is who God is. The nature of love is to express itself toward others. God pours His love into the heart of anyone who will receive it. Look back to John 3 above. Jesus wasn't sent to condemn anyone. The world was already under condemnation, but Christ came to rescue any who will receive it. The only ones who remain under condemnation are those who love the darkness of sin and reject the love of Christ.

Do you love darkness? Chances are, if you are reading this book, you do not. You are looking for an escape from the darkness of addiction and sin. God is not evaluating the depth of your sin to determine if you are worthy of love. God expressed (and continues to express) His love because that is who He is. Love desires to express itself to others.

Let me reiterate this important truth. God doesn't love you because of who you are. He loves you because that is who He is. God doesn't love you because of what you have done. God loves you because that is who He is. God loves you, and if you will receive it, you will experience the unconditional love of God.

God loves the gambling addict because He is love.

God loves the drug addict because He is love.

God loves the prostitute because God is love.

God loves the homosexual because He is love.

The Love of God

God loves the porn addict because He is love.

God loves the murderer because He is love.

The sin is irrelevant. The depth of our failure is irrelevant. Sin is of the flesh, but new life is of the Spirit. God is calling you out of the flesh and into His presence in the Spirit. When you succumb to temptation and fall, God's nature has not changed. God is still love and love never fails.[22]

Your righteousness was never dependent upon you. You have the righteousness of Christ. He took your sins to His account and credited the righteousness of God to your account. (See 2 Corinthians 5:21). Your right standing with God is dependent upon Christ. His work on the cross doesn't fail just because you do. When you fail, turn back to Christ and be led back into the Spirit. In the Spirit, our life can only be pure. In the flesh, our life can only be impure.

God is not disappointed when you sin or blow it. Disappointment is when we fail to meet someone's expectation. Disappointment would assume that God expected one thing and we did the opposite. God sees the end from the beginning and according to scripture, God fashioned your days before you were born. That means He knew you would sin before you did. When you sin, God already knew you were going to blow it, and He has already set His plan in motion to guide you back to the right way. Then He uses your failures to teach you how to completely depend upon Him.

If God was going to give up on you when you blow it, He would have foreknown your failure and wouldn't have bothered to call you into grace. Instead, God delights in taking people who have no strength to overcome and make them into victorious believers. The greater your weakness, the greater God's power rests upon you and the greater He glories in your success. Your success is not based on your abilities, but the power of God to transform your life into His image.

Never buy into the lie that God rejects you. Never believe the lie that God only has a limited number of chances or that your failure creates anger with God. Sin is judged but you are rescued. Does God hate the sin? Absolutely. That is why He died on your behalf. Consider **Romans 3:23-26**

---

[22] 1 Corinthians 13:8

<sup>23</sup> for all have sinned and fall short of the glory of God,

<sup>24</sup> being justified freely by His grace through the redemption that is in Christ Jesus,

<sup>25</sup> whom God set forth *as* a propitiation by His blood, through faith, to demonstrate His righteousness, because in His forbearance God had passed over the sins that were previously committed,

<sup>26</sup> to demonstrate at the present time His righteousness, that He might be just and the justifier of the one who has faith in Jesus.

Sin is an assault against God. Anything that contradicts God's character or nature is a violation of the law and must be judged. God will never violate His own law, for to do so would go against His own nature – and this is not possible. God can't change.

Therefore, since God loves us, but sin must be judged, He bore the penalty of sin on our behalf. Keep in mind that we were created by God and in the image of God. Through sin, we violate our design and fall short of God's glory that we were intended to reflect. Instead of being the image of God's glory, sin reduces us to the corruption of the flesh.

Without violating the law or His nature, God justified us while remaining just. If our legal system has a judge that winks at violators, we consider that person to be a corruptor of the law. Order cannot exist where the law is not enforced. If someone breaks the law and stands before a judge, does their good outweigh their bad? Suppose a car thief stands in court and says, "I was caught in the act stealing the car, but look at all the good I have done in other areas. I take care of my family. I give to charity. I helped an old lady change her tire."

He could name thousands of good deeds, but what does the law say? You stole and you are guilty. All the good you have done does not erase the crime. The penalty must be enforced.

The same is true for God's law. God must be just, and the law demands justice for each sin we have committed. Yet because God loves us, He bore the penalty of the law on our behalf, and once that was accomplished on the cross, God declared us to be just because we put our trust in Jesus' work on the cross. Now God can remain just *while* justifying those He loves. The law wasn't violated; it was satisfied to the letter.

You are now free from the law and its penalties. You are now free to enjoy the loving relationship with God as He intended from the beginning. When you blow it, look again to the cross and put your confidence in what Christ has done. When you are trying to overcome the weaknesses of the flesh, look to the cross and have confidence in what Christ has done.

According to 2 Corinthians 3:18, we are transformed into Christ's image as we behold His glory. The secret of overcoming is found in learning how to stay focused on Christ. The one who understands the love of God and His forgiveness and mercy begins to learn how to receive that love. As that person receives love, they begin to love God in return. As we grow in love, our focus becomes Christ centered and the Spirit within us begins the transforming work in our lives.

As you learn to look to the cross, faith will mature, your focus will change, and God has promised to transform your life. It's time to stop trying to change yourself and rest in Christ.

Never allow guilt to overcome you. Never believe that God has turned His back on you. Believe God. He has declared your acceptance in Christ, and nothing can nullify the word of God. God has declared that His work has been completed on your behalf. Now it's time to allow the Spirit to transform your outward life into the image of the inward man God has created within you according to His own image. You are sanctified in Christ. Now allow God to transform you into that completed work. Trust in Christ's work on your behalf.

When you fall short, return your focus to the completed work of Christ and begin the process of transformation. When you blow it again, return your focus to Christ, rest in grace and be transformed. The grace (or unearned favor) of God is your life. Rest in grace, don't labor in the flesh. Learning to rest in Christ can be a long process, but as you learn to rest in Him, what seems like a mountain today will be a stepping stone in the future.

Believe in what God has declared for you. The reality of life in the Spirit overcomes the mirage of the flesh. The flesh can only dominate the life of the one who trusts in its power. Be transformed by the power of God!

# Is Addiction Physical, Mental, or Spiritual?

In many ways, addiction is a combination of physical, mental, and spiritual problems. People with destructive behaviors tend to claim, "I'm just wired this way." Studies on the brains of sexuality have indicated that brain development plays a vital role in behavioral normalcy. While some people are born with certain tendencies in their physical makeup, there are almost always life-events that push people into a destructive form of behavior.

The brain has an amazing ability to 'rewire' itself in response to traumatic events. A person can recover from many brain injuries to regain normal functions, even when the damaged area cannot fully heal. The brain rewires itself to bypass the trauma.

Substance addictions create physical changes in the brain that rewire behavior or try to compensate for over-stimulation. This is why drug addicts have a harder time getting high after repeated drug usage. And why it is so difficult to break free. Because the pathways of the brain have been altered, substance stimulation is now needed in order to get to as close to normal as possible. Higher doses are needed to get above normal and feel high.

In sexuality, similar problems exist. Studies have shown that the anterior hypothalamus, the portion of the brain that responds to sexual stimulation, is under developed in homosexual men, and often over developed in sexually addicted individuals. The limbic and right prefrontal areas of the brain have become dysregulated, often due to a childhood trauma or overstimulation during development.

When a sexual or emotional trauma or over-stimulation is introduced during the childhood development years, sexual issues can have life-long consequences. This comes out in varying behavior patterns, but in each case, a lack of behavior control is almost always involved to some degree.

My goal here is not to be technical, but to introduce the concept that truly you are 'wired that way'. Many addictions are in fact physical problems. A child introduced to pornography (such as I was) is over stimulated repeatedly in the development years. The result is an overdeveloped hypothalamus that has become dependent upon that stimulation. A child subjected to sexual abuse is either stimulated sexually, or develops a defensive coping mechanism where they detach emotionally or find other ways of dealing with the trauma in their patterns of thinking.

As a result, dysfunctions emerge throughout life. Some of these dysfunctions don't emerge until the late teens through early adulthood, or when relationships are formed.

Substance addictions may have a greater affect during development years, but even in adulthood, if something is introduced into the brain that is foreign, the brain will attempt to compensate by redirecting brain patterns or attempting to block the unnatural stimulation in order to regulate it. This is also why many psychiatric drugs lose their effectiveness over time.

Regardless of the cause, the problem is the same. A physical challenge stands between you and recovery. You now have to overcome the way you are wired. This is not easy. In many cases it is almost impossible. I say impossible; however, your thought patterns will change, but only after you are in the recovery stage.

And herein lies the problem. Your mind can't rewire itself because it has become dependent upon the behavior or substance for stimulation. Yet it can't begin to rewire its thought patterns until *after* a new way of thinking has been established. This is why so many addicts fail to have lasting behavior change. The change must alter the behavior, yet the natural mind only has behavior as its mechanism of change.

Often times, it's easier to overcome substance abuse issues than it is to overcome behavioral problems. Substance alters the brain in ways that are normally temporary, but behavior addictions stem from the brain itself.

Addiction is a physical problem with a spiritual solution.

# The Flesh is Subject to the Spirit

Understanding the challenge we face serves to guide us toward the true source of help. We must get out of the endless loop of trying to use self-dependent behavioral changes as a tool against self-destructive behaviors. For most people this cannot work. However, the new spirit of life we have been given has the power to take control of the will and bring it under subjection instead of allowing the will to be ruled by the cravings of the flesh. Look at **Romans 8:13-15**

> [13] For if you live according to the flesh you will die; but if by the Spirit you put to death the deeds of the body, you will live.
> [14] For as many as are led by the Spirit of God, these are sons of God.
> [15] For you did not receive the spirit of bondage again to fear, but you received the Spirit of adoption by whom we cry out, "Abba, Father."

Most people try to overcome their weaknesses through efforts of the flesh. By flesh, I'm referring to human effort. The flesh is our physical bodies and the way of thinking that was born from human nature. When we attempt to overcome destructive behaviors produced by the flesh with less destructive behaviors of the flesh, we are still living in the flesh. We are asking the flesh that is controlling us to help us regain control. It's like asking an oppressive dictator to help us overthrow his wicked regime. At best, he will use our trust to bring us under greater bondage.

Let's step back again and look at what we previously discussed. If you have an addiction, it is rooted in the flesh. The flesh is wired for sin because it is fallen and born under the sin of Adam. (See the Victorious Christian Life for a deeper explanation.) We have a physical problem that is real and controls our ways of thinking and behaving to some degree. The answer is not to exchange one addiction for another. Some try to adopt religion, hobbies, or other distractions in an attempt to shift our addiction from one thing to another. Depending on the depth of the addiction, some will have a certain amount of success. Many make temporary change, but later slip back into harmful behaviors.

It has been said that the sex addict cannot change. This attitude comes from observing sexual behaviors that come out as predatory actions. In his own strength, the child molester can't change. The rapist cannot change. The porn addict cannot change. Why? Because they are wired this way. They cannot change themselves, but does this mean that change is not possible?

Is Addiction Physical, Mental, or Spiritual?

I once looked at myself and said, "I cannot change." I had tried and failed to break free, but my desires hunted me down and recaptured my mind each time I denied its demand to satisfy the cravings of the flesh. I could never get outside of its control. I could not change. It was a physical problem that affected my mental state. When the flesh called, it took over my mind and I could do nothing but obey.

Yet something did change when the Lord entered the picture. Through the Spirit, the deeds of the flesh were put to death. The mind may be controlled by the brain, but the mind is a separate entity from the brain. The brain cannot change itself, but the mind can change. Then the brain must repattern its way of reacting to accommodate the spiritually minded person.

This sounds odd until you realize that the mind is not dependent upon the brain. Humanistic science denies this truth, but many evidences challenge the assumption that the brain is the mind. Spiritual life is not dependent upon the flesh, nor is the spiritually minded man subject to the whims of a physical brain.

To illustrate this truth, I'll use a real life and verifiable example.

There are documented cases where people have been brain dead but were completely aware of their surroundings. Let's consider what is probably the most remarkable near death experience to date – the surgery of singer / songwriter, Pam Reynolds. Every stage of her death was completely monitored by the doctors and presents one of the most compelling stories I've ever heard.

In 1991, Pam developed dizziness and loss of motor skills. After a CT scan, it was discovered that she had a very large aneurism in the center of the lower part of the brain. It was in one of the most inaccessible areas to operate. She was told repeatedly that it was inoperable, but she found a doctor at Barrow Neurological Institute who agreed to perform the risky operation.

According to Dr. Robert Spetzler, in order to perform the operation, all life and brain functions had to be stopped. Her body temperature was dropped to 50 degrees Fahrenheit and the blood was drained completely from her brain. Dr. Spetzler explains, "In order to perform this operation, the brain can't just be asleep; we need all metabolic activity to stop in the brain. Every measurable activity was completely stopped. There was no neurological activity whatsoever."

Pam remembers everything up until the time she was put to sleep – the gurney going down the hallway and the administering of the anesthesia. "I never saw the doctor before the surgery began," she explained. She went to sleep and doesn't remember anything until she heard a guttural sound grinding the top of her head. She looked to see and suddenly had the view from above the doctor's shoulder.

Though she never saw the tools before the operation, she was able to describe what looked like drill bits and the doctor sawing her skull with what appeared to be a dentist tool. She said she was surprised because she thought it would look more like a saw and blade. She then heard a nurse say, "We have a problem. The arteries are too small."

The doctor then directed the nurse to drain the blood from the other side. She was witnessing the procedure to drain the blood from the brain.

According to the surgeon, Dr. Spetzler, "There was no way she could have heard or seen anything at that stage of the operation." To monitor brain activity, plugs are put into the ears that produce a constant clicking in order to see if the brain responds to sound. These plugs would both block out sound from the ears, and alert the surgeon if the brain should respond to the sounds. He continues, "I don't have an explanation for it. I don't know how it is possible, considering the physiological state she was in."

So what does this near death experience have to do with addictions? It is to simply point out the truth that though the brain normally controls the mind by feeding its thought patterns to it, the mind is actually separate from the brain. This proves that it is possible to think independently from the dictates of the flesh.

The Bible teaches that man has been created with a body, soul, and spirit. Consider these two passages:

**Hebrews 4:12**
For the word of God *is* living and powerful, and sharper than any two-edged sword, piercing even to the division of soul and spirit, and of joints and marrow, and is a discerner of the thoughts and intents of the heart.


**1 Thessalonians 5:23-24**
[23] Now may the God of peace Himself sanctify you completely; and may your whole spirit, soul, and body be

Is Addiction Physical, Mental, or Spiritual?

preserved blameless at the coming of our Lord Jesus Christ.
$^{24}$ He who calls you *is* faithful, who also will do *it*.

Understanding that we as Christians have the power to be Spirit led is of vital importance. Because of our ignorance of this basic truth, we feel helpless as our body controls our soul, and the soul is cut off from our spirit. We become flesh driven and our minds and soul are completely submitted to the dictates of the flesh. Yet when we come to Christ, God divides the spirit from the soul so that we now are able to live and think independently of our flesh-driven old nature.

In the natural state before Christ, our flesh was the focus. As a newborn, when we felt hungry, we cried out and were fed. When we felt discomfort, we cried out and were changed. Self-gratification became the central goal of our life and as we matured, we found new ways to gratify the demands of the flesh. The flesh desires something sinful, so we sin in order to please the flesh. Because we have always answered to the flesh, it was our master.

In Christ everything changes. The old nature was put to death in Christ and we were born as a new creation. God gives us an incorruptible nature that desires only one thing – to live according to its nature. Because the new nature is the life of God, it delights in godliness, holiness, and craves intimacy with God. But there is a problem. We haven't learned how to put to death the deeds of the body.

For our entire lives, we have listened to the flesh and our normal tendency is to satisfy its cravings – whether good or bad. Our minds have always drawn its inspiration from the flesh and even a new Christian drifts back into that way of thinking after the newness of Christ has faded from their emotions. If we don't learn how to look to the Spirit, by default we are looking to the flesh. Since that is all we have ever known, we automatically lean on our old ways of thinking.

When we become a new creation in Christ, our spirit born through Adam is divided from our soul and put to death. We now have a body of flesh, soul (which is our personality, mind, and emotions), and our spirit. The spirit is now a new creation, but the body and soul are still conditioned to think according to the old nature. The flesh is born into that nature and can do nothing but sin unless it is brought under subjection.

And that is the present day struggle you are having. The body still cries out to be gratified, and stands in defiance of anything but selfishness. If the flesh is allowed to rule, it will drive you to sin. If allowed to go unchecked, it always seeks to enthrone itself and bring the soul under its rule. The spirit we have been given is incorruptible because it is of God, and the new spirit cannot sin. Consider these passages:

**1 John 3:9**
Whoever has been born of God does not sin, for His seed remains in him; and he cannot sin, because he has been born of God.

**1 Peter 1:22-23**
[22] Since you have purified your souls in obeying the truth through the Spirit in sincere love of the brethren, love one another fervently with a pure heart,
[23] having been born again, not of corruptible seed but incorruptible, through the word of God which lives and abides forever,

These passages are not saying that you cannot sin through the flesh. They are teaching that God has placed a new nature within you that cannot sin because it is incorruptible.

When the flesh is in control, the spirit is cut off and the flesh rules the soul – which is also the mind. Your brain is of the flesh, but your mind can either be in the flesh or in the Spirit. Let's bring in a few scriptures to explain. Look first at **Colossians 3:1-3**
[1] If then you were raised with Christ, seek those things which are above, where Christ is, sitting at the right hand of God.
[2] Set your mind on things above, not on things on the earth.
[3] For you died, and your life is hidden with Christ in God.

Add to this **Romans 8:13**
For if you live according to the flesh you will die; but if by the Spirit you put to death the deeds of the body, you will live.

Is Addiction Physical, Mental, or Spiritual?

In other words, the Spirit has the power to bring the flesh under subjection, but you have the power to set your mind in the Spirit or allow it to be ruled by the flesh. When your mind is ruled by the flesh, you are serving sin. In the Spirit the mind naturally serves righteousness. Consider **Romans 7:25**

I thank God -- through Jesus Christ our Lord! So then, with the mind I myself serve the law of God, but with the flesh the law of sin.

Can you will your flesh into subjection? No. You can only submit yourself to the Spirit of God and trust His word to bring your flesh under subjection. Through the Spirit you put to death the deeds of the flesh. The old nature may be dead, but the deeds of that old nature live in the flesh. Let's bring in one more passage to bring further clarity to this truth, **Romans 7:22-23**

[22] For I delight in the law of God according to the inward man.

[23] But I see another law in my members, warring against the law of my mind, and bringing me into captivity to the law of sin which is in my members.

This is a wonderful truth! The inner man, that new nature born of God, delights in righteousness. The body, however, serves the law of sin. Its desire is to be served and have its cravings satisfied according to the law of sin; therefore, it wars against your mind, trying to bring you back under bondage so you will think and act in ways that fulfill the lusts of the flesh.

You don't have to submit to the flesh. If you have put your faith in Christ, you are a new creation and have the power to live as a child of God. When you are walking in the Spirit, you aren't fighting off the craving to sin because your spirit doesn't want to sin. You will delight in what is good and reject what is of the flesh. But if your mind is in the flesh, the cravings of the flesh will rule over you and bring you back into bondage to serve sin.

The flesh seeks to cut off the new man so it is excluded. The spiritual man rejects the flesh. The Spirit and the flesh are perpetually at war with each other and can never agree.[23] The new man, that spirit

---

[23] Galatians 5:17

placed within you as your new nature, is born of the Spirit. You either walk according to your new nature and rule the flesh, or you walk according to the deeds of the flesh and it rules your mind. Your soul is either controlled by the flesh or by your spirit. It can't be ruled by both or shared by both.

Ideally, your mind is on the Spirit. God's Spirit is always communing with your spirit to reveal the will of God. When your mind is in agreement with your spirit, your spirit reveals to the mind what is of God, then your mind (part of your soul) brings your flesh and body under subjection and then you are an instrument of God's righteousness.

The opposite is often the case in most Christians. The spirit is neglected, so the flesh wars against the mind and easily captures it, because it has no directive from the Spirit. The mind then cuts off the revelation of the Spirit but instead submits to the flesh. Then the body becomes an instrument of unrighteousness that serves sin.

With this understanding, let's revisit the problem of addiction. The flesh/body has been wired for self-serving but destructive behaviors. There is a physical problem that makes the cravings of sin harder to resist and thus creates these addictive behaviors. When the body is in control, the mind is ruled by a brain that has been mis-wired for addiction. The tendency is too strong for the will, and though we may resist for a while, the cravings hammer at the will until we desire relief more than resistance. Then we return to the addiction, gratify our flesh, and become a servant to sin. We can do no other, for sin is greater than the strength of our will.

In Christ something changes. The mind is set on spiritual things, where Christ is. Our spirit is *always* in submission to God and is receiving revelation from God; therefore, the mind on the Spirit naturally acts according to its new nature. Even if we don't understand what takes place in the spiritual side of us, we still receive strength and help. Consider **Romans 8:26**

> Likewise the Spirit also helps in our weaknesses. For we do not know what we should pray for as we ought, but the Spirit Himself makes intercession for us with groanings which cannot be uttered.

Even in the midst of our weakness, God's Spirit is interceding for us and receiving the revelation of God and the power of God. Not only that, consider this amazing passage from **1 Corinthians 2:12-16**

> [12] Now we have received, not the spirit of the world, but the Spirit who is from God, that we might know the things that have been freely given to us by God.
>
> [13] These things we also speak, not in words which man's wisdom teaches but which the Holy Spirit teaches, comparing spiritual things with spiritual.
>
> [14] But the natural man does not receive the things of the Spirit of God, for they are foolishness to him; nor can he know *them,* because they are spiritually discerned.
>
> [15] But he who is spiritual judges all things, yet he himself is *rightly* judged by no one.
>
> [16] For "who has known the mind of the LORD that he may instruct Him?" But we have the mind of Christ.

Through the Spirit, we receive all the things of God that have been given to the believer as a gift of love. We already have the power of God to overcome, but we don't realize that power because we are looking at faith through the eyes of flesh and therefore can't see. The flesh cannot receive the things of God, nor can it see what has been freely given.

You cannot know these things until you are walking in the spirit. Rather than doing something to become more spiritual, we are called to walk in the Spirit so we can receive what has already been given to us. You don't earn this. You cannot change your life in order to receive it. Instead, believe God and allow the things He has given you to overcome the things you previously could not change.

Take special note of the last verse. You and I have the mind of Christ. You already have all you need to live the victorious Christian life, but this only comes by revelation of the Spirit. And we can only receive the revelation of the Spirit when we are walking in the spirit.

So then our flesh is wired for sin, but the body is subject to the Spirit. The flesh cannot overcome the Spirit of God, nor can it overcome our new spirit, who is born of God. The only thing the flesh can do is turn your mind away from the things of the Spirit and put your focus back on the flesh. The real battle is learning how to walk in the Spirit so we are drawing from the mind of Christ and the power of God, instead of drawing from the flesh and subjecting ourselves again to the things God has delivered us from.

The reality of the Spirit is greater than the mirage of the flesh. The flesh only looks real because we walk in the flesh and are persuaded of its power and worth. But the truth is, all that we see will be done away with and what we don't see will one day be all that remains. To understand this, let's bring in two other passages.

**2 Peter 3:10-11**

[10] But the day of the Lord will come as a thief in the night, in which the heavens will pass away with a great noise, and the elements will melt with fervent heat; both the earth and the works that are in it will be burned up.

[11] Therefore, since all these things will be dissolved, what manner *of persons* ought you to be in holy conduct and godliness,

**2 Corinthians 4:17-18**

[17] For our light affliction, which is but for a moment, is working for us a far more exceeding *and* eternal weight of glory,

[18] while we do not look at the things which are seen, but at the things which are not seen. For the things which are seen *are* temporary, but the things which are not seen *are* eternal.

If what is seen will one day be dissolved and come to nothing, and the eternal, that which is not seen by eyes of flesh, is all that will remain, what is the mirage and what is reality?

The mirage, the passing flesh rooted in the passing world, cannot overthrow what is real – that which is born of God. Your flesh cannot rule your spirit, but your spirit *does* have the power to rule your flesh.

Your addiction, which may be born out of a physical problem, whether incurable or not, it cannot stand against the flesh. Your brain does not have the power to rule your mind. Your mind has the power to bring the physical brain under subjection and force it to live according to the dictates of the inner man.

The only reason this is not realized is because the individual has never learned how to walk in the Spirit and submit all things to God.

And God delights in glorifying Himself by overcoming the impossible. The incurable addiction is broken through the Spirit.

Even if your body craves sin and demands to have its addiction gratified, it has no power to force its will upon your mind. If your mind is in Christ, the addiction can only call from a distance. It is when we begin walking in the flesh that the cravings regain their hold. And when that happens, the solution is simple. Step into the Spirit again. Let's conclude this chapter with a powerful verse from **Galatians 5:16-18**

> [16] I say then: Walk in the Spirit, and you shall not fulfill the lust of the flesh.
> [17] For the flesh lusts against the Spirit, and the Spirit against the flesh; and these are contrary to one another, so that you do not do the things that you wish.
> [18] But if you are led by the Spirit, you are not under the law.

If you are in the Spirit, the lust of the flesh has no power, for you are no longer under the law of sin. Though you may be aware of these cravings, they have no power unless you set your minds back in the flesh. Verse 17 says, "so that you do not do the things you wish." A little is lost in translation. In Greek (the language the Bible was written in) literally says, "So that you do not produce what you desire."

The message is that in the Spirit, you cannot be driven by desires because if you are led by the Spirit, you aren't under the law. Keep in mind that the law is the knowledge of sin,[24] produces sin,[25] strengthens sin,[26] and the law of sin works in our body of flesh to war against our minds.[27] Also consider **1 Corinthians 15:56**

> The sting of death *is* sin, and the strength of sin *is* the law.

Through the grace of God, we are set free from the law, and therefore the strength of sin is broken. You are now free to live in liberty and not be ruled by sin. It has no power over you.

---

[24] Romans 3:20
[25] Romans 5:20
[26] Romans 7:8
[27] Romans 7:23

Though the temptation may remain in our flesh (including the brain), it has no power until we submit to the flesh. In time, our new way of thinking according to our new nature will rewire our patterns of thinking and lessen the temptations. The flesh is still the flesh and is tied to our old nature; therefore, we will never be completely freed from temptation or our tendency to succumb to addiction. But it will become easier to resist.

Do not let your liberty give way to a new temptation. When we see the power of the flesh being broken, it's tempting to toy around with our old ways and allow our guard to drop. Yet sin crouches at the door, waiting for the slightest opportunity. That is when people fall back into their old addictions. Yet the solution should be easier the next time around, for we now understand the way of escape.

Never grovel in failure or allow Satan to beat you down with guilt. There is no condemnation in Christ. Simply turn from your fleshly way of thinking and again live according to the Spirit. God is not angry. He has made the way of escape and is leading you toward it. If anything, our failure reveals the truth that we are completely dependent upon the power of God and His unearned favor. His power must be our strength. Our own strength can never give us true power to become godly.

# Dying to Live

**Romans 6:4-7**

<sup>4</sup> Therefore we were buried with Him through baptism into death, that just as Christ was raised from the dead by the glory of the Father, even so we also should walk in newness of life.

<sup>5</sup> For if we have been united together in the likeness of His death, certainly we also shall be *in the likeness* of *His* resurrection,

<sup>6</sup> knowing this, that our old man was crucified with *Him,* that the body of sin might be done away with, that we should no longer be slaves of sin.

<sup>7</sup> For he who has died has been freed from sin.

Anyone who is in Christ is a new creation. The old man that once ruled their life is dead. He has been crucified with Christ. Has been, not will be. This is a truth that eluded me for more than two decades. I lived as though I were trying to defeat a sin nature, not knowing that it had already been defeated.

Let me give an example of what this passage is addressing. An elephant trainer once explained his methods of keeping elephants under control. The young elephant was tied to a strong tree. He could not pull free because he lacked the strength. Over time, he stopped pulling against the tree knowing he could not break the rope and certainly couldn't uproot the tree.

Once the elephant learned to quit pulling, the trainer would move the elephant to a strong pole in the ground. It would be difficult, but as the elephant grew, he could have pulled up the pole. But since he had been conditioned by the tree, when he felt resistance, he quit pulling against the pole.

In time the elephant was moved to a rod. The rod had no strength to restrain the massive elephant, but because he believed the rope bound him, he stood passively and waited without resistance. The rope had no power to hold him, but because he believed it did, the elephant submitted to its restraint.

This is what has happened to the Christian in bondage. The power of sin has been broken, but we are so conditioned to it that we believe in its power to bind us. It calls and ties us to the temptation that overcomes us. We feel powerless to resist or break free, and because we are mentally bound to the lust, we stand there helplessly until we give in to its demands.

You are not bound to sin or temptation, for he who is in Christ has been set free from sin. Let me note that when the Bible uses 'he' in the general sense, it is like 'man' in the general sense. It applies to mankind as a whole – both men and women.

Let's stop for a moment and reiterate what it means to be in Christ. Becoming a Christian is not a work of human effort. We don't convert to Christianity; we are changed into a new nature. When the message of freedom in Christ is preached, the Lord draws us. The message is that we were bound to sin because we were born into sin. All have sinned and fallen short of the glory of God we were created to be partakers of. We are designed to be united with God and have our life bound up in His life.

Sin is the barrier, for sin is anything that rejects or rebels against God or His nature. You cannot be united with God if you are in rebellion against God. Since we were born into a sinful nature, our natural tendency is to serve our selfish nature and reject anything, including God, that challenges our right to self-gratification. I go into this topic in greater detail in Simple Faith and The Victorious Christian Life, so I'll only briefly summarize here.

Since sin is a violation of the law, the law demands sin to be punished. This is clearly seen even in man's law. When someone breaks the law of our society and is arrested, the law demands justice. No one stands before the judge and says, "Look at all the good things I have done. I've given to charity, helped the elderly, fed my family, and done many more good things than bad."

If they did, the judge would just shrug and say, "None of that matters. You broke the law." You aren't punished because your bad outweighed your good. You are punished because you broke the law. Even if you do everything right but break one law in one area, you will be penalized for breaking the law. So it shouldn't be surprising that when it comes to God's law, sin is a breaking of the law and is judged – regardless of any good we may have done. The law has been broken and you are guilty.

Yet because God's desire is for mercy, He bore the penalty of sin on our behalf. Let's let **Philippians 2:5-8** explain:

⁵ Let this mind be in you which was also in Christ Jesus,
⁶ who, being in the form of God, did not consider it robbery to be equal with God,
⁷ but made Himself of no reputation, taking the form of a bondservant, *and* coming in the likeness of men.
⁸ And being found in appearance as a man, He humbled Himself and became obedient to *the point of* death, even the death of the cross.

So though Jesus was God, He became flesh and submitted Himself to the death of the cross in order to pay the penalty for your sin. This is the message of salvation. The Bible goes on to say that we are saved by grace (God's unearned favor) through faith. Faith is believing what God has declared and putting our trust in Him.

Our redemption is looking to the cross and believing that what Jesus did is the love of God expressed toward us. God saw your sin and said, "Because I love you, I will take the punishment of the law for you so you can be freed from the law of sin." He then was nailed to the cross with the wrath of God against sin, and now judgment has been satisfied.

You now have to put your trust in what He has done. Once you recognize the gift of God offered through the cross, you must believe in Him, release your old life in the flesh, and receive the new life of the Spirit. God then accounts you as dead in Christ as though you were punished, but also gives you the righteousness of Christ. And once you believe God, you are accounted as righteous, apart from anything you have done. What's more, God gives you a new spirit and a new nature – one that has its life in God's Spirit. You literally become a new creation, old things have then passed away, and now all things are new and of God.[28]

It is important to understand and receive this basic truth. This is where the Christian life begins. This is also where the battle begins.

Before Christ, the flesh ruled, and because you only had a sinful nature, there was nothing to challenge the flesh. Once you receive Christ, you are given a new nature and the old nature is crucified – put to death in Christ. This is an accomplished fact and not something

---

[28] 2 Corinthians 5:17-18

we are trying to accomplish ourselves. Your old nature is dead. Not will be crucified, but has been crucified.

The flesh remains, but the sinful nature that ruled the flesh is dead. Yet because the flesh is accustomed to being in charge, it still demands to be served. Your mind is like the elephant tied to the fragile rod. You may think you are bound, but in truth, the ties that bind you have already been broken. Your mind is conditioned to passively allow sin to reign, but once you learn to set your mind on the things from above, you'll recognize the freedom you have in Christ. Let's go back to Romans and dig in further. Look at this wonderful truth from **Romans 6:11-14**

[11] Likewise you also, reckon yourselves to be dead indeed to sin, but alive to God in Christ Jesus our Lord.

[12] Therefore do not let sin reign in your mortal body, that you should obey it in its lusts.

[13] And do not present your members *as* instruments of unrighteousness to sin, but present yourselves to God as being alive from the dead, and your members *as* instruments of righteousness to God.

[14] For sin shall not have dominion over you, for you are not under law but under grace.

You are dead to the flesh but alive to the Spirit. You must now reckon – or believe enough to account yourself dead to the flesh, but alive in God. What seems like bondage to sin is actually our submission to it. Sin tells us that we are under its rule, but it is actually intimidating us into submission. Yet we have the power to not submit to sin, but to submit to righteousness. We'll then experience the freedom of the peace we have always had, but never realized.

If you are in Christ, sin has no dominion over you. Do you believe this? Sometimes we have to constantly remind ourselves of this truth until it sinks in and becomes part of our way of thinking. Sin seeks to rule and have dominion, but God seeks to lead and give freedom. One seeks to oppress; the other calls us to submit.

The primary thing standing between you and overcoming is your faith in the flesh and lack of faith in the finished work of Christ. You do not have to overcome; you must learn to trust in His power to overcome as you learn to walk in the Spirit – where victory has already been given.

# You have been raised with Christ

This is a topic that speaks for itself. I am going to recite a number of scriptures that I hope will speak to your heart. These are spread throughout the New Testament, but when drawn together, they paint a wonderful picture of our resurrection power through Christ. **1 Peter 1:3**

> Blessed *be* the God and Father of our Lord Jesus Christ, who according to His abundant mercy has begotten us again to a living hope through the resurrection of Jesus Christ from the dead,

Through the cross, you died. By death, you were freed from the requirements of the law and its claim over your life. While that is good news indeed, the greater news is that you are now a new creation. Take to heart the greatness of the promise in **2 Corinthians 5:17**

> Therefore, if anyone *is* in Christ, *he is* a new creation; old things have passed away; behold, all things have become new.

If you are in Christ, you are not the same person you were. The old passed away because it died in Christ. You have been crucified with Christ. Past tense. Now all things are new. Present tense. The new creation is in Christ – incorruptible and free from sin and untouchable by sin's temptations. Let's revisit **1 John 3:9**

> Whoever has been born of God does not sin, for His seed remains in him; and he cannot sin, because he has been born of God.

Let's add to this a passage from **1 Peter 1:22-23**

> [22] Since you have purified your souls in obeying the truth through the Spirit in sincere love of the brethren, love one another fervently with a pure heart,
> [23] having been born again, not of corruptible seed but

incorruptible, through the word of God which lives and abides forever,

Let these passages sink in for a moment. Something happens at your conversion. Being converted is not just a mental agreement with the ideology of Christianity. Indeed, there are many who claim the Christian faith in principle only, but this is not who we are talking about. Jesus said, "Unless you are born again, you cannot see the Kingdom of Heaven."[29]

Just believing the Bible is true does not make one a Christian. There must be faith – the answer of God's call to surrender to the truth of God where we release ourselves into God's hands. He takes our life and places us in Christ. This means we have been forgiven of sin because our transgressions were washed away by the blood of Christ. Our old nature has been crucified through the cross of Christ, and we are raised as a new creation through the resurrection of Christ.

Once someone is born again – or is raised with Christ, they are a new creation. At this moment two things happen. God places His Holy Spirit within us and gives us a new nature, born out of that Spirit. We are literally a new person. The new man is born of God, finds its life in God, and because it is of the Holy Spirit, that new life is incorruptible. It cannot sin, for it is born of God. The flesh has no power over the new creation God places within us.

That which sins is destined to die. It cannot live, for once sin occurs, the pronouncement of death is upon it. The soul that sins must die.[30] The only way to purge sin, as we have seen, is death. That is why salvation cannot be found in any other name than Jesus Christ.[31] Only Jesus died on our behalf and paid the penalty of sin. Unless a life is in Christ, death remains the penalty of sin. In Christ we died, and only in Christ has that payment already been made. All who are outside of Christ are still under condemnation and remain destined for the wages of sin – judgment and death.

Our new nature cannot sin. It is impossible. If it could, it wouldn't have its life in God. Anything that sins inherits the wages of

---

[29] John 3:3
[30] Ezekiel 18:20
[31] Acts 4:12, John 14:6

Dying to Live

sin, which is death. But we have eternal life, cannot sin, and our inner man cannot be corrupted, for sin cannot enter Christ.

If this is true, it begs the question, "If I am new, my old nature is dead, and my new nature is immune to sin, why do I still sin?"

This is one of the great mysteries of faith. A mystery that God has revealed in His word, but most misunderstand. Some say the Christian cannot sin. Others say we are merely sinners saved by grace. While yet others make the claim that each time we sin, we fall under condemnation again, and are in need of another salvation.

Eternal life can't die. Those who teach that we lose salvation, are saved again, and lose salvation yet again, simply do not understand the scriptures. Can our inner man die and still remain incorruptible? Can we say that our inner man sins and must be cleansed while remaining consistent with scripture? None of these can be. If life is eternal, it cannot die. If our spirit is incorruptible, it cannot sin. Confusion arises when the line between the flesh and the Spirit is blurred in our understanding.

The flesh cannot be redeemed. All sin is through the flesh. All that is affected by sin must be destroyed. God doesn't put lipstick on a corpse and call it clean. The corpse must be buried. And we see this truth throughout scripture.

We are called to abandon what is destined for destruction and lay hold of what is eternal. The eternal is a gift God is offering, but this gift can only be held in empty hands. This means God is asking us to let go of what is dying so He can take it out of the way and replace it with true life. There is a cost to discipleship. That cost is losing the world and all we have invested into the world. If anyone loves the world, the love of God is not in him. Consider **1 John 2:15-17**

> [15] Do not love the world or the things in the world. If anyone loves the world, the love of the Father is not in him.
> [16] For all that *is* in the world -- the lust of the flesh, the lust of the eyes, and the pride of life -- is not of the Father but is of the world.
> [17] And the world is passing away, and the lust of it; but he who does the will of God abides forever.

Everything our eyes see is passing away. Why love what is dying at the expense of that which cannot die? The world is not our focus. As your life changes, this becomes a testimony to others who are struggling in the same battles. The world around you becomes your mission field, yet the world itself is not your focus.

You will be going behind the enemy's lines to proclaim that God has rescued any who will receive it by faith. It isn't your work, but God's. Your life will become a trophy of grace that will give hope to others! The world will not accept the gift, but individuals seeking escape will receive it. And no one can reach those in the pit better than someone who has been there.

A disciple is one who has abandoned the world and all its empty promises and taken hold of Christ. A disciple is someone who sees the reality of the eternal, and this causes them to realize the falsehood of the temporal. Each believer must understand that dying to this life is how we receive the new life. We don't keep both. Consider the words of Jesus in **Luke 14:26-30**

> [26] "If anyone comes to Me and does not hate his father and mother, wife and children, brothers and sisters, yes, and his own life also, he cannot be My disciple.
> [27] "And whoever does not bear his cross and come after Me cannot be My disciple.
> [28] "For which of you, intending to build a tower, does not sit down first and count the cost, whether he has *enough* to finish *it* --
> [29] "lest, after he has laid the foundation, and is not able to finish, all who see *it* begin to mock him,
> [30] "saying, 'This man began to build and was not able to finish.'
> ...
>
> [33] "So likewise, whoever of you does not forsake all that he has cannot be My disciple.

The call of discipleship is a call to forsake all. We are called to forsake dreams, hopes, possessions, relationships, and any pleasure that does not come from God's hand. Does this mean that we abandoned wives and children? No, but it does mean that we cannot choose the will of others over the call of God. In reality, it is those rooted in the world who abandon the relationship. Knowing this to be a possibility is something we must consider before stepping out by faith.

52

I met a Jewish pastor who chose to follow Christ. His family threatened to disown him if he didn't abandon Christ. He chose Christ and was disowned and disinherited. Some of his family later came to Christ, but others did not. He willingly forsook all, leaving the relationships into God's hands.

If you are in a similar situation, this might be something you have to face. Many of the addict's relationships are based on mutual addiction. If one chooses to be free and the other does not, the addict is now faced with a choice. Do we accept the dying lifestyle in order to maintain a relationship? Or do we let go of the relationship and put all into God's hands? When we do so, reaching out to our old relationships will be a journey into the world on a rescue mission, but not all are willing to let go of the world.

Many don't count the cost, begin to build their life on Christ, and when the cost becomes great, they abandon the call and settle for the world.

The truth is that the cost is small in the eternal scheme of things, but great in this life. Or at least it appears great. Those who view life through the eyes of the world will value the things of the world. And then the cost seems too high. But when someone sees the reality of the eternal, they recognize the answer to Jesus' question, "What profit is there if someone gains the whole world but loses their soul?"

There is no profit. To invest our lives into something destined for ashes is a foolish investment. But the world looks at the Christian, and because they cannot see the eternal, it seems utterly foolish to abandon all the world offers to lay hold of what they think is religion.

It's not mere religion. It is to lay hold of Christ with the understanding that the eternal is what is real, and the world is the mirage.

Don't expect the world to understand faith. Don't expect your friends and family to understand your call. Don't even expect the church to understand your call into the Spirit. Any who view life through the eyes of flesh will scoff at the idea of true faith.

People will give lip-service to faith, but when it comes to the cost, the truth of their focus will be shown. "You have to be practical," they will say. Most people trust God up to the point where they recognize they are becoming truly dependent upon Him. Once someone realizes that God is leading them into a life where they cannot meet their own needs and cannot protect themselves should God fail them, most will turn back.

When the way of the cross puts us into a position where God is stripping our confidence away, most will turn back. When the things in this life that we value begin to fall away, our affections are either torn from the flesh, or we cling to our earthly affections and let go of Christ. That is also when the cost is too great. We would have begun the tower, but not able to finish. Not seeing God's provision ahead of time would have then been too big of a step of faith to obey. Losing things we once thought were valuable would then have been too big of a step of faith to obey.

When friends and family say you are being a fool, that is when Jesus says, "Anyone who loves father, mother, husband, wife, or anyone else is not worthy of Me." When your own soul cries out to turn back, that's when Jesus says, "He who does not hate his own life also, cannot be My disciple."

It's a hard calling. It's not hard because the work is burdensome, but because God leads us out of all confidence in the flesh and into complete confidence in Him. Some will be called to abandon careers; others will not. Some will be called to sell all and go into missions; some will not. Some will see their families turn on them; others will see families follow them into the call.

This is where it becomes impossible to tell someone how to walk by faith. What God does in the life of a faithful man or woman will be a great testimony of His faithfulness, but it is not the example of how God works in every life. You follow the call of God as He reveals Himself to you. And that does not come by making a decision based on your own will. It comes through knowing Christ so intimately that you recognize His voice and follow where He leads.

It all begins with the call to die. Die to your life, count the cost, and look to Christ without ever looking back. Then you will see each step of God's leading. Count the cost and then die to this world – and your own life. Then you'll see true life.

Let go of what is passing away and experience true life in the Spirit. This is how we experience the abundant life now, and see the joy of God's promises yet to be fulfilled. When we stand in eternity, the things of this world will be a forgotten mirage. How then ought we to live at this present time?

# Dividing the Flesh from the Spirit

One of the most overlooked and misunderstood truths of the Christian life is the dividing of the soul from the Spirit. Before we dig into the power of this division, let's look at **Hebrews 4:12**

> For the word of God *is* living and powerful, and sharper than any two-edged sword, piercing even to the division of soul and spirit, and of joints and marrow, and is a discerner of the thoughts and intents of the heart.

Many have read this passage, but still miss the main point of it. Let's look at how the body, soul, and spirit work to produce either righteousness or sin in our lives.

Before coming to Christ, each person has a spirit. From the very beginning, God breathed into Adam the spirit of life. This was human life, not eternal life. Yet God offered Adam two choices – partake of the tree of life or turn from God and partake of the tree of the knowledge of good and evil.

The tree of life is God-dependence. It is to put one's trust solely in God alone. God is life, blessing, knowledge, and our righteousness. The tree of life is to look to God as our complete sufficiency and acknowledge our dependence on Him.

The tree of knowledge is to look at one's self. It is the desire to be independent from God. The temptation was (and still is) to be like God. Satan tempted Eve by saying, "If you choose this way, you will be like God. You will be able to know good and evil, determine right from wrong. You can be independent from God."

Once both Adam and Eve chose this path, their eyes were indeed opened. While they were God focused, all they saw was the righteousness of God and He was their covering and provider. Once their eyes were upon themselves, they became self-conscious. The first thing they saw was their own nakedness and shame. Becoming aware of good and evil actually revealed shame, not righteousness. Adam's righteousness was never in himself – it was in God. Once that was removed, shame overtook him because he was no longer God-focused.

Anytime we are self-focused, we are sin-conscious. Once we are conscious of sin, we either try to cover it with our own efforts, deceive ourselves into thinking we are good, or are swallowed up in our own guilt and shame. Even the one who deludes himself does not eliminate his guilt. He simply deceives himself into not acknowledging it. Even the self-righteous person allows guilt to slip in when their self-efforts fall short. In God's eyes, our efforts always fall short, but man can convince himself that he is good even while being aware of the evil present with him.

Just as Adam tried to cover his shame with leaves, those who don't understand grace or have never received Christ try to cover themselves instead of allowing God to cover them with His righteousness.

God placed a curse on the forbidden fruit when He said, "Of every tree you may eat, but of this tree you may not eat. The day you eat of it you will surely die." Life is in God and from God; therefore, true life cannot exist apart from God. Once Adam rebelled, his spirit was cut off from God and spiritually he died. The process of physical death began once he was alienated from God, but spiritual death was instantaneous.

Adam received a fallen nature once he became a partaker of sin. All were born into that nature inherited from Adam, but everyone sins by their own volition. The tendency to sin comes from our sinful nature, but judgment comes from our own act of rebellion after the likeness of Adam.

Something wonderful happens when a person comes to Christ. Jesus is called 'the second Adam.' All sin passed through the first Adam and into the world – including into the lives of every person. Jesus is the second Adam that all must pass through to escape sin. Adam is the parent of sin; Jesus is the parent of righteousness.

This goes back to the topic of dying to self. When we come to Christ, we are crucified with Christ and the old nature is buried with Him in baptism. It is now dead. Just as Christ was raised incorruptible, we also are raised in Christ as an incorruptible new man.

The new life you have in Christ was born of God through His Holy Spirit. It is an eternal spirit born into a new nature. The old has passed away and the new nature is incorruptible. It has to be incorruptible because it abides in Christ. Nothing *of* God can sin and nothing *in* God can sin. Sin cannot abide in God's presence. This is why 1 John 3:9 says that those who are born of God cannot sin.

This is where the Christian life can get confusing if you don't understand what is being taught – and if you don't understand the difference between the soul and the spirit. That which is born of God cannot sin. This applies to you, the addict. If you are in Christ, your new nature cannot sin, but your flesh can. Now let's draw the Apostle Paul's struggle into this explanation. Look at **Romans 7:22-25**

<sup>22</sup> For I delight in the law of God according to the inward man.

<sup>23</sup> But I see another law in my members, warring against the law of my mind, and bringing me into captivity to the law of sin which is in my members.

<sup>24</sup> O wretched man that I am! Who will deliver me from this body of death?

<sup>25</sup> I thank God -- through Jesus Christ our Lord! So then, with the mind I myself serve the law of God, but with the flesh the law of sin.

Can a Christian sin? Since we still have a physical body, yes. But we cannot sin through the new man. We can only sin through the flesh. The new nature (or new man) is born of God and cannot sin, but if we live according to the flesh and not according to the Spirit, we will sin. In fact, in the flesh sin will overtake our minds and bring us into captivity.

Let's digress for a moment to the passage we first read in this chapter. The word of God is able to divide the soul from the spirit. Why does the spirit and the soul need to be divided?

When you were living under your old nature, it was ruled by the body. Our bodies, which are corrupted by sin, crave to be served. This comes out in many forms of sin, not just addiction. However, an addiction is a great example of how the power of the body's cravings demand to be gratified. Before Christ, your body demanded to be served and it employed your soul to do its bidding. Your soul consists of your emotions, desires, and ways of thinking. Because your soul took its direction from the body, it in turn ruled over your natural spirit, rendering it useless. Our spirit and soul became one and inseparable. The spirit is useless in that when Adam chose sin, the spirit was cut off from God and now lives only to serve the soul – man's selfish desires.

The Bible says that faith comes by hearing the word of God, or message of Christ.[32] We hear, believe, and put our trust in Christ. Once we surrender to Christ, the Holy Spirit accomplishes two things in us. The spirit is divided from the soul and is put to death. In man's spirit is our old nature. It is cut away, buried with Christ, and we are given a new spirit with a new nature. Now old things have passed away and all things are of God (review 2 Corinthians 5:17). We are a new creation, born of God, and our new nature is now incorruptible.

If our new nature cannot sin, why do Christians struggle and commit sins?

Reread the passage of Paul's lamentation over his own tendency to sin. Sin dwells in the flesh, but wars against our minds trying to bring us back into captivity. Notice what is clearly implied. You are free, but sin tries to recapture what it has lost – your mind and will. It cannot recapture your spirit, for that is of God and cannot be corrupted. But it can capture your mind and attempt to bring your soul back under slavery to its passions.

If you are in the Spirit, the flesh has no power. If you are in the flesh, you are living according to your old dead works. The flesh is dead in its sins, but you do not have to abide in the mire any longer. However, you will drift toward that way of thinking unless your mind is in the Spirit. And that can only happen if you understand the difference between the flesh and the Spirit. Take to heart this passage from **Galatians 5:16-18**

[16] I say then: Walk in the Spirit, and you shall not fulfill the lust of the flesh.

[17] For the flesh lusts against the Spirit, and the Spirit against the flesh; and these are contrary to one another, so that you do not do the things that you wish.

[18] But if you are led by the Spirit, you are not under the law.

Before Christ, there was no war. Sin might have warred for total control of your mind, but there was no opposing force to stand against it – except your will, and your will is no match for sinful passions. After Christ, you have a new nature and spirit. Sin still

---

[32] Romans 10:17

resides in the flesh and it wars against your mind, trying to dominate your soul and employ your will to overrule the nature of your new spirit.

In Christ, by nature you will do righteousness, for that new nature is born of God and receives instructions from the Spirit of God. In the victorious Christian life, your spirit receives the revelation of God. As you meditate on the word of God and renew your mind, what is being revealed to our spirit enters the mind and renews your soul. The soul then rules the body and you present your body as an instrument of righteousness to God to do His will. (See Romans 6:12-13).

If we allow sin to rule our soul, it recaptures our minds and then uses it to rule our bodies to obey its lusts. Righteousness comes from the inner man and goes outward to the body and into the world around us. Temptation begins from the outside and works its way in. We receive temptation from the world around us. Sin in our flesh craves that temptation and causes the body to lusts after it. Then sin wars against our minds in order to capture it and use our will to submit the body to obey its lusts.

What seems like a powerless obsession to serve our cravings is actually a process that we can intervene to stop. The problem is that most people start with behavior and try to change the man. But behavior is actually the last thing to fall into place. If we are living according to the inner man, the Spirit puts to death the deeds of the old nature, the soul is brought under subjection to our spirit (which delights in righteousness by nature), and our body is brought under subjection. The right behavior is the natural result. Consider **Romans 8:13**

If you live according to the flesh you will die; but if by the Spirit you put to death the deeds of the body, you will live.

Who puts to death the deeds of the body that is ruled by sin? Not you. It is God's Spirit that does this when we are spiritually minded by focusing on Christ. And this is why we struggle to bring our lives into a godly standard. We tend to begin with behavior, and while we might have limited success, once we encounter a passion that is more determined than our will, failure is inevitable. Our will is limited by human strength, but passions and lusts are fueled by an old nature that weakens our will. Though the nature is now dead, the deeds and passions born from that nature remain in the flesh – for the flesh will not be changed until we are changed into Christ's likeness after this life is over.

True change comes when we see our soul beginning to live according to our new nature instead of the works born out of old nature. This is explained in **1 Thessalonians 5:23**

Now may the God of peace Himself sanctify you completely; and may your whole spirit, soul, and body be preserved blameless at the coming of our Lord Jesus Christ.

Once again we see the spirit, soul, and body mentioned, but this time in reference to sanctification. Sanctification means to be purified and set apart for God. The Bible says that we are already sanctified through Christ (Hebrews 10:10). This is referring to the inner man.

This truth is vitally important. You have been sanctified – past tense. God has purified you and set you aside as an heir of His eternal kingdom. Now He calls you to live according to your new nature and learn to depend solely upon Christ. As you do so, your soul will be drawn into the sanctified life that you already have in your spiritual life.

There is a reason why God did not completely remove our flesh. The greatest journey of the Christian life is the process of learning how to wean ourselves off of self-dependence and onto Christ-dependence. God is teaching you how to overcome through trust.

The Bible says that the weakness of the law was the flesh. Anything depending upon the weakness of human nature will ultimately fail. Even those who thought they were righteous under the law crucified Christ, for though they didn't have immoral behaviors, sin came out in ways they didn't recognize as sin.

Human nature cannot overcome sin. Nor can the flesh overcome the sin that was born out of the old human nature. Deliverance only comes through the Spirit, for when we are walking in grace by faith, we have removed the only thing preventing righteousness – our own weakness.

Dividing the Flesh from the Spirit

# Trust in Forgiveness

In the Old Testament, God ordained the sacrifice of atonement. According to the New Testament, the atoning sacrifices served a few functions that were fulfilled through Christ. First, the animal sacrifices were never intended to take away sin. They were a yearly reminder of the wages of sin, which is death.[33] More importantly, the sacrifice was a symbol that pointed to the coming Christ, who would become the Lamb of God – the final sacrifice for sin.[34]

Once Christ fulfilled the law, there was no longer a need for sacrifice or the old system of law. These were intended to lead mankind to Christ, but once Christ came, that which pointed to Him is no longer needed. Let's look at the amazing picture of forgiveness as taught in the Old Testament and fulfilled for us in Christ.

The lamb was the symbol of atonement. Each year, at the time of Passover, God's people would bring a lamb without blemish to the priest. He would inspect the lamb to determine if it was faultless. Once approved, the sinner would lay their hands upon the lamb's head to symbolically transfer their sins to the lamb. The lamb would be slain and the blood would be sprinkled on the altar to symbolically cover their sins. The sins were never done away with – they were covered for one year.

When Jesus lived, He perfectly fulfilled the law and then offered Himself up as the spotless Lamb of God – the perfect atonement for sins. Unlike the symbolic sacrifice in the Old Testament, Jesus did not merely cover sin for a year, but He removed sin completely. The Bible says that all the wrath of God against sin was poured out on the cross. One of Jesus' last words were, "Tetelestia." Most Bible versions translate this into, "It is finished," but the actual Greek word means, "The debt has been paid." The debt was finished because all that was owed had been paid.

When Jesus ate the last Passover supper with His disciples, He explained that the Passover meal was symbolic of what He was about to do. The bread was His body, broken for our debt, and the wine

---

[33] Romans 6:23, Hebrews 10:3-4
[34] Galatians 3:24-25

represented His blood that would be poured out as an atonement for sin. Consider the words of **Colossians 2:13-14**

> [13] And you, being dead in your trespasses and the uncircumcision of your flesh, He has made alive together with Him, having forgiven you all trespasses,
> [14] having wiped out the handwriting of requirements that was against us, which was contrary to us. And He has taken it out of the way, having nailed it to the cross.

Notice that the sins against us were not merely covered; they have been taken out of the way. All sin has been paid on the cross. All sin. The sins you committed in the past were paid at the cross. When they were paid, they were all future sins, yet they were laid to Jesus' account on the cross. The sins you have recently committed and will commit were also future sins when Jesus paid for them. This means they are paid in the past tense for you – even before you committed them.

This is very significant, for when you wallow in guilt and shame, you are denying that Jesus paid your debt. While you are crying out, "Please forgive me," Jesus has already declared, "Father forgive them," on the cross. And it was Jesus who said, "The Father always hears Me." That prayer was answered when Jesus spilled His blood for your sins.

This is why the Bible says that Jesus became sin for you that you might become the righteousness of God in Him. (See 2 Corinthians 5:21) Whose righteousness makes you right with God? It is not your righteousness, for the Bible says that all our righteous acts are filthy in God's sight.[35] Your righteousness can NEVER make you right with God. Nor is it your sins that prevent you from experiencing the joy of fellowship with God. Even in the Old Testament, God declared that He made people righteous by covering them with His own righteousness. Look at **Isaiah 61:10**

> I will greatly rejoice in the LORD, My soul shall be joyful in my God; For He has clothed me with the garments of salvation, He has covered me with the robe of righteousness, As a bridegroom decks *himself* with ornaments, And as a bride adorns *herself* with her jewels.

---

[35] Isaiah 64:6

Trust in Forgiveness

The Old Testament saints kept the law as an act of faith in what God would one day provide in Christ, and when they believed, God credited them with His righteousness. See Genesis 15:6. God has never changed. You aren't righteous because of what you do for God or because of your efforts to measure up to a godly standard. You are righteous for only one reason. You believe in God's gift of grace, and God rewards you with His own righteousness. Grace simply means the unearned favor of God.

When you sin, can your failures nullify the righteousness of God? You can fall short of your own righteousness, but you can never overthrow the righteousness of God.

The Bible says that our sins were laid to Jesus' account on the cross. If you sin, does that change the fact that God laid your sin upon Jesus? Or does the fact that sin exists in your life nullify the righteousness of God that now covers you like a robe?

While it is true that you cannot enjoy the fellowship of God while you are active in sin, your failure doesn't negate God's success. We enjoy God's fellowship in the Spirit, but we sin when we step into the flesh. All sin is in the flesh, yet all righteousness is by the Spirit. That means when we sin, we have stepped out of God's best for us and are dabbling in the old life of death. The old life has nothing but consequences and worthless wages, but in the Spirit we have perfect fellowship and peace.

To get a deeper understanding of the war between the flesh and the Spirit, I explain this in detail in The Victorious Christian Life.

One thing we must allow to sink into our hearts is that forgiveness is not dependent upon our abilities to measure up. Forgiveness is a gift of God that is received by faith. Your sin was paid 2000 years ago. Believe this truth and when you sin, thank God for what He has done. Certainly we are sorry for our sins, but we must not allow shame and guilt to take root in our hearts. Have faith. Believe what God has already declared. You are the righteousness of God. Your failure cannot overthrow this truth because it is not dependent upon you.

You are not righteous because you did anything right. You are righteous because of what Jesus accomplished. Your sin has no power to nullify the work of Christ. Believe in God's forgiveness and allow God to account you as righteous.

The natural question that arises is, "What if I fall back into pornography?" Your fall has no power to overcome Christ's power and righteousness. It was never your righteousness, but Christ's credited to your account.

"What if I fall back into an alcoholic binge?" Get off the ground, look to the cross and thank God for His eternal mercies.

"What if I prostitute myself or steal for money when I allow cravings to overcome me?" Your flesh has been crucified with Christ. It is already dead. Believe God's declaration. Read **Romans 6:5-14** and take this to heart:

5 For if we have been united together in the likeness of His death, certainly we also shall be *in the likeness* of *His* resurrection,

6 knowing this, that our old man was crucified with *Him,* that the body of sin might be done away with, that we should no longer be slaves of sin.

7 For he who has died has been freed from sin.

8 Now if we died with Christ, we believe that we shall also live with Him,

9 knowing that Christ, having been raised from the dead, dies no more. Death no longer has dominion over Him.

10 For *the death* that He died, He died to sin once for all; but *the life* that He lives, He lives to God.

11 Likewise you also, reckon yourselves to be dead indeed to sin, but alive to God in Christ Jesus our Lord.

12 Therefore do not let sin reign in your mortal body, that you should obey it in its lusts.

13 And do not present your members *as* instruments of unrighteousness to sin, but present yourselves to God as being alive from the dead, and your members *as* instruments of righteousness to God.

14 For sin shall not have dominion over you, for you are not under law but under grace.

When your flesh overcomes you and your actions are contrary to who you are in Christ, what is the answer? It is to reckon or account yourself dead to sin. Step out of the sin, reckon that part of your old life as dead (which it is) and set your focus on the life you have in Christ.

Sin shall not have dominion over you! Do you believe this? Until this is your confidence, you will have a faithless mindset that is ruled by sin. Yet when you believe what God has declared, God has promised to transform your behavior into the person you are in Christ.

If you get drunk, are you a drunkard? Not if you are in Christ. That drunkard is dead. Stop dragging the dead body of flesh around and acting like the dead man you once were. By the Spirit we put off the deeds of the old man. He is dead, but the deeds of the body must now be put to death with the old nature. In Christ you are sober and righteous. The inner man is incorruptible (review again 1 Peter 1:23 and 1 John 3:9).

When you sin, claim the truth of these passages. Thank God that the new nature you have is incorruptible and that sin cannot have dominion over you. Believe in God's power to fulfill His word and begin walking as the new person God has created. If you fall again, shake off the flesh and begin walking in the Spirit. That is who you now are, but the cravings of the flesh desire who you once were.

We have it backwards in our Christian culture. We try to become righteous by what we do and not by faith in what Christ has done. We try to change our behavior by submitting our will to the flesh in the hopes that the flesh can accomplish something that is against its nature. The truth is that we put off the flesh and put our minds upon the Spirit. If we don't believe we are who God says we are, how can we expect to live according to that new nature?

If when we fail, we wallow in guilt and shame, how can we expect to separate ourselves from the deeds of the flesh? Let's revisit the passage where the sacrifice of Christ is compared to the sacrifices of the Old Testament. There are a lot of life-changing truths here, so I want you to read these carefully without skipping over them. Begin with **Hebrews 10:1-3**

<sup>1</sup> For the law, having a shadow of the good things to come, *and* not the very image of the things, can never with these same sacrifices, which they offer continually year by year, make those who approach perfect.

<sup>2</sup> For then would they not have ceased to be offered? For the worshipers, once purified, would have had no more consciousness of sins.

³ But in those *sacrifices there is* a reminder of sins every year.

There is one key point I want you to keep in mind as we move ahead. If someone's sins were paid, they should have had no more consciousness of sin. If the animal sacrifice could have taken away sin, they should have no longer been conscious of sin. Keep in mind that this was written about people just like you and I. After the sacrifice, they would have made mistakes and committed sins. Yet, if the sacrifice had been sufficient, they would not have been conscious of sin.

The old sacrifice could never have made the individual perfect. A perfect sacrifice would take away sin and should also take away guilt and shame. The worshiper would then no longer be under the guilty conscience of sin. Don't let this slip far from your mind as we go on to read **Hebrews 10:17-23**

¹⁷ *then He adds,* "Their sins and their lawless deeds I will remember no more."

¹⁸ Now where there is remission of these, *there is* no longer an offering for sin.

¹⁹ Therefore, brethren, having boldness to enter the Holiest by the blood of Jesus,

²⁰ by a new and living way which He consecrated for us, through the veil, that is, His flesh,

²¹ and *having* a High Priest over the house of God,

²² let us draw near with a true heart in full assurance of faith, having our hearts sprinkled from an evil conscience and our bodies washed with pure water.

²³ Let us hold fast the confession of *our* hope without wavering, for He who promised *is* faithful.

This is referring to the New Covenant. In Matthew 26:28, Jesus said, "For this is My blood of the new covenant, which is shed for many for the remission of sins."

We are in that new covenant. And what is one of the key promises of the New Covenant? "Their sins and lawless deeds will I remember no more." The one who believes should hold to the confidence of our hope in Christ without wavering. The law could not justify because people could not keep themselves in perfection. Now the weakness of the law, our flesh, has been removed as a barrier and no longer can we fall short of the perfection of Christ. It is not based on our perfection, but God's promise. He is the guarantee of the New Covenant. His guarantee cannot fail even if we fall short.

If you are in Christ, you are in the New Covenant and because sin has been taken out of the way, God does not remember them or take them to your account. They are forgiven AND removed. When did this happen? It happened on the cross. It does not happen when you confess. It does not happen each time you sin, grovel in guilt, and seek repentance. Repentance is a part of the Christian life, but repentance does not mean begging God for forgiveness. To do so would be to deny that Jesus has already paid your debt.

The word 'repentance' means to change the mind. It also means to change direction. Repentance is to acknowledge that we are sinning because we are walking in the flesh, so we change our minds away from the flesh and set our minds on the things of the Spirit. We change directions by stopping our pursuit of the flesh and begin walking in the fellowship we already have in the Spirit.

Forgiveness has already been granted. Stop groveling in the flesh and instead put your trust in what God has already done.

God saw your sins before you were born. He foreknew you and nailed your sins on the cross, regardless of how depraved they may be. He already knew them and paid the debt before you committed them. So why do you hide your head in shame? God has already lifted your head and seated you with Him at the table of fellowship. Stop crawling under the table and rejoice in who you are in Christ. This is not pride or arrogance. It is faith in God's power to defeat sin, bear your shame in His own body, and make you righteous by His power.

Don't deny God's power to overcome your weakness. Believe God and be accounted as righteous. It is an accomplished fact. All you must do is receive it by faith.

When you blow it, put your eyes on Christ. When guilt points an accusing finger at you, put your eyes on Christ. When shame tries to cover you, put your eyes on Christ and rejoice like the spotless bridegroom who is covered with the robe of God's righteousness. Rejoice like the spotless bride adorned with the jewels of Christ's glory.

This is why there is no more consciousness of sin. Those under the Old Covenant had to yearly be reminded of God's provision for sin, but could never rejoice in the realization of being fully redeemed. We have this amazing gift in our very grasp!

When you fully understand God's grace – unearned favor – you will no longer have a consciousness of sin, for you will be focused on the gift of righteousness you have received. Rather than constantly having to seek forgiveness, you will become Christ aware instead of sin-aware.

Adam and Eve were naked and unashamed when they were in fellowship with God. But they thought gaining the knowledge of good and evil would allow them to choose good. Instead that knowledge took their eyes off of God's righteousness, and their eyes were drawn to their inability to become righteous. They hid from God because they were sin-conscious. Since they were now self-focused, they were ashamed. They were never able to live in complete perfection, but it didn't matter until they became sin-conscious.

In Christ, we have that curse reversed. Once again we have the freedom to be Christ-focused, and when we are, we lose the ability of being sin-aware. The knowledge of good and evil is put to death and we look to Christ as our only source. In Him, all things are good and the flesh loses its ability to lure us back into temptation. This is how we overcome sin.

Sin is the selfish cravings of the flesh that demands we turn our eyes back to ourselves and try to determine what is good and evil based on how it pleases the flesh. Walking in the Spirit is when we are looking to Christ for life, righteousness, holiness, our provision, and the one who satisfies us with the abundance of His goodness.

As you focus on Christ and the provision of His unending favor, the sins you committed fall from view, and guilt cannot be found, for there is no remembrance of sin. The sacrifice of Christ has satisfied justice and we are no longer aware of our shortcomings. They don't matter anyway, for faith is not what we do for God or our ability to measure up. Faith is trusting completely in Christ and knowing all things are of Him, by Him, and for Him.

Guilt and shame may rise up to distract us from our focus, but like all temptations, they fall away as we focus on Christ, the Author and Finisher of our faith. Whether our sins were committed yesterday, today, or the distant past, they have already been overcome

68

by the blood of Christ and we overcome them by trusting in His power. How long ago or how recently we have fallen is irrelevant. We overcome through Christ.

God has promised that we are changed into His likeness as we behold His glory. It isn't you who transforms your behavior. It is God's transformation power as you trust in Him. Believe and trust in His accomplished work. Then you have no more consciousness of sin, for you are abiding in the righteousness of Christ.

Let me summarize this chapter with **Hebrews 9:12**
Not with the blood of goats and calves, but with His own blood He entered the Most Holy Place once for all, having obtained eternal redemption.

The Bible is once again showing how the earthly ordinance served only to point us to the heavenly accomplishment of Christ. After the lamb was slain for the sin of the person, the earthly High Priest would go into the holiest place of the Jewish temple and sprinkle the altar with the blood. Once again I want to emphasize that this was a yearly reminder, for man's efforts can never take away sin. This had to be done every year of the person's life.

How many times does Jesus atone for our sin in heaven? He did this one time. Jesus entered into the holiest throne of heaven and atoned for all since. He did this once for all, having obtained eternal redemption for us. When does eternal end? It doesn't. The work of Christ was accomplished. It only had to be accomplished once, for His work is eternal and cannot be undone.

When you sin, the altar does not have to be sprinkled again with Christ's atoning blood. Forgiveness and redemption was accomplished once for all.

Do you have to be forgiven each time you sin? No. Redemption was accomplished once for all. If you had to be forgiven each time you sinned, then the blood would have to be applied over and over. Jesus doesn't get nailed to the cross for each sin or each sinner. It was one work, accomplished one time, for all sins and all people.

Rest in what Christ has done and let the Spirit transform your outward life into His finished work.

# Renewing Your Mind

The world is constantly drawing your attention toward temporal things. In fact, that is the heart of addiction – temporary pleasure. While our selfish desires promise pleasure and freedom, the pleasure is for only a moment and instead of freedom, we are drawn into bondage. An addiction is a never-ending quest for gratification. Yet temporary pleasures can never satisfy but instead enslave us to our flesh and the world.

Thankfully, Jesus set the captives free. When Jesus began His ministry, He opened the book of Isaiah and read, "The Spirit of the LORD is upon Me, Because He has anointed Me To preach the gospel to the poor; He has sent Me to heal the brokenhearted, To proclaim liberty to the captives And recovery of sight to the blind, To set at liberty those who are oppressed; to proclaim the acceptable year of the LORD."

Jesus closed the book and said, "Today this scripture is fulfilled in your hearing."

Interestingly, the section where Jesus read from goes on to speak of God's judgment, wrath, and the overthrow of this world's system. But Jesus didn't read on because His first coming was to proclaim your freedom in Christ, deliverance from sin, and the acceptable year of the Lord.

You are accepted by God through Christ. You are freed from sin through Christ. God's purpose in Christ is not to judge people in their weakness or oppress those who are captive to sin. He proclaims our liberty. Look at **2 Corinthians 3:17-18**

[17] Now the Lord is the Spirit; and where the Spirit of the Lord *is,* there *is* liberty.

[18] But we all, with unveiled face, beholding as in a mirror the glory of the Lord, are being transformed into the same image from glory to glory, just as by the Spirit of the Lord.

I've referred to verse 18 throughout this book, but the point must be driven home until Christ is formed in you. You are not only freed from sin, but God has given you His transforming power so your outward behavior is conformed to His image. God doesn't automatically make you Christ-like. He has allowed this world to be a challenge to your faith so you learn to trust in His power – even against overwhelming odds.

Everything in this world may stand against you, but if God is for you, nothing else shall stand. All God is asking is for you to look to Him.

God isn't asking you to change yourself or your behavior. He is asking you to look to Him, believing in His power to transform your behavior.

When God's people wandered through the desert during their journey toward the Promised Land, serpents invaded the camp and began biting people. The deadly venom was certain death. God did not drive the serpents away, instead He asked Moses to do something strange. Moses was instructed to make a brass serpent, place it on a pole, and erect it in the midst of the camp. If someone was bitten, they were told to look to the serpent on the pole and they would be delivered from the snake's venom.

You know what happened to those who said, "How can looking at a pole save me?" They died from the venom. The pole itself had no power to do anything. It was the symbol of God's provision. Those who looked to the pole were delivered by God's power. It wasn't the pole, nor was it their effort. It was their faith in God's word.

Jesus said, "Just as Moses lifted up the serpent in the wilderness, so must the Son of Man (Jesus) be lifted up," referring to the cross of crucifixion. When someone looks to Christ, just as God intervened to save His people in the wilderness, God also intervenes to rescue that person from the poison of sin.

This world is filled with the venom of sin and temptations that constantly bite at our soul. It is no small miracle that anyone can live a godly life. Yet even though we are surrounded by trials and temptations, God empowers us to live victoriously in Christ as we journey through the wilderness of this world.

You cannot rescue yourself from sin. But God has already rescued you. Look to Christ and you will be changed into His likeness.

The Lord has allowed us to journey through a snake infested world for one reason – to reveal His power to us and in us. When you begin to change into His likeness, the world around you will wonder. They will think it strange that you no longer sin with them or they'll wonder how you can lose the taste for temptation. Many will scoff

**Renewing Your Mind**

and point at your failures, some will criticize you, but others will see your testimony of His power and seek this for their own life.

Then you will stand back in amazement. Not long ago you were defeated by sin, and now God has taken your sin-filled life and transformed you into a trophy of grace. And the Lord delights in taking the least worthy and least capable among us and revealing His grace through them. The reason? That no flesh should glory in God's presence. God is not looking for those who can say, "I did it," but for those who know they cannot do it and yet are willing to allow God to make them into a new creation.

Once we think we have earned grace or done something to make ourselves righteous, we have stepped into the flesh and have limited the power of God in our lives.

God will allow you to struggle until you learn complete trust and complete dependence upon Him. And if you think you aren't worthy, you are just where you need to be. God loves sinners and delights in transforming them into the righteousness of Christ.

Inevitably, when the grace of God is taught, some will say it sounds like sin is being accepted. Quite the opposite is true. You are forgiven and delivered so you can receive something greater. If you sin again after being forgiven, does God still account you as righteous? Yes, for it was never your righteousness. Your righteousness is not your own, but is the righteousness of Christ credited to you. Does Christ's righteousness cease just because you sin? Certainly not.

It is possible to live for this world after coming to Christ, but why would someone who has escaped from the condemnation of a dying world want to live in that system of death? Why would we want to live for death when we have life in our very grasp? Why would we invest our lives in a world that is passing away and forfeit our inheritance of God that will never pass away? Yet some people do.

Disregarding the gift of Christ because some people will abuse it is not the answer. People also attempt to exploit legalistic religious practices and systems for their selfish motives. The real benefit of forgiveness is that we have escaped the lusts of this world and now have the promises of God. For the rest of our lives we are learning to abide in Christ so we can fully experience and share in His glory. Consider again **2 Peter 3:10-11**

> [10] But the day of the Lord will come as a thief in the night, in which the heavens will pass away with a great noise, and the elements will melt with fervent heat; both the earth and the works that are in it will be burned up.
>
> [11] Therefore, since all these things will be dissolved, what manner *of persons* ought you to be in holy conduct and godliness,

Godly conduct comes through abiding in Christ and allowing His Spirit to work in our lives. Certainly we can invest in a world that will one day be dissolved, but look at the joy before you. Your temptation will rise back up and promise you the world. As you regain control of your life, temptation will take new forms and attempt to use your new confidence in Christ as though it will protect you in sin. Most people will fall on occasion – not because temptation is too strong – but because they feel they can escape.

Temptation is anything that calls us to look away from our life in the Spirit and focus on our flesh or this passing life. Certainly we have to make a living, but we don't have to live as though our hope is in gaining possessions or pleasures.

Your focus will naturally drift toward the flesh unless you are active in renewing your mind. Look at **Romans 12:1-2**

> [1] I beseech you therefore, brethren, by the mercies of God, that you present your bodies a living sacrifice, holy, acceptable to God, *which is* your reasonable service.
>
> [2] And do not be conformed to this world, but be transformed by the renewing of your mind, that you may prove what *is* that good and acceptable and perfect will of God.

In the past, your body was the instrument of sin to serve your passions and desires. Now you have the right to present yourself to God and discover the perfect will of God. That will includes the promise, "It's your Heavenly Father's good pleasure to give you His kingdom." God wants you to rein with Him. God wants you to receive is perfect love.

Renew your mind through prayer, the word, and fellowshipping with God in the Spirit. Don't allow temptation to rob you of God's best by exchanging the promise of God for a moment of sin.

You have been set free. Rejoice in that freedom. Fellowship with God in the Spirit. Be transformed into the image of God by beholding the glory of Christ.

God's love is never ending. As you recognize His love, it will transform you more than all the rules, religious practices, and regulations man can dream up.

When you fall, rejoice in that you are already forgiven and turn back to the fellowship of heaven. God has made the way before you even fell. As you get the right attitude toward grace, the power of temptation will begin slipping away and your love for God will emerge. Never run from God or try to make up for wrongs. Trust in the truth that God foreknew your sin and paid the price before you fell. Look to Him and be changed!

If you would like to know more about walking in the Spirit, I encourage you to read, The Victorious Christian Life: Living in Grace and Walking in the Spirit. The ebook version is 99 cents.

## Below are other books written by Eddie Snipes:

The Promise of a Sound Mind : God's plan for emotional and mental health

Simple Faith: How every person can experience intimacy with God

I Called Him Dancer – Christian Fiction

You can connect with Eddie Snipes in the following ways:
Personal Website: www.eddiesnipes.com
Ministry site: www.exchangedlife.com
Email: eddie.snipes@gmail.com
Twitter: @eddiesnipes

Made in the USA
Las Vegas, NV
11 February 2023

67322914R00042